HUSBAND PARTICIPATION IN MATERNAL HEALTHCARE

HUSBAND PARTICIPATION IN MATERNAL HEALTHCARE

Dr. Gyanvati

KALPAZ

First Published, 2019
Published by
Kalpaz Publications
C-30, Satyawati Nagar,
Delhi – 110052
Ph.: 011-47034999, 9811692060
www.kalpazpublications.com
E-mail: kalpaz@hotmail.com
Printed at: G. Print Process, Delhi

Cataloging in Publication Data—DK
Courtesy: D.K. Agencies (P) Ltd. <docinfo@dkagencies.com>

Gyanvati, author.
Husband participation in maternal healthcare / Dr. Gyanvati.
pages cm
ISBN 9789353240622

1. Maternal health services—India. 2. Husbands—India.
I. Title.

LCC RG965.I4G93 2019 | DDC 362.198200954 23

Contents

Foreword

Men and women have differential healthcare needs, though they have equal right to healthy living. However, in Indian socio-cultural milieu, majority of women have hardly enjoyed any reproductive rights. Chronic malnutrition, anaemia, ignorance of their health needs, multiple and repeated pregnancies, have impacted maternal as well as child health severely. The UN Women has claimed that every day, around the world, 830 women die from preventable ailments related to pregnancy and child birth. Compound effects of gender discrimination, among others, have systematically restricted their access to health services.

Safe motherhood and related aspects of maternal and child healthcare have been important agenda items, globally as these are reflected in Millennium Development Goals and now Sustainable Development Goals. In this regard, the World Health Organization has initiated several programmes to enhance male involvement in promoting maternal and neonatal health. Husband participation in maternal healthcare is thus a recent phenomenon that is increasingly recognized as an effective strategy to improve access to sexual and reproductive healthcare services and guarantee right to health among women. Since mid-1990s, there has been an increased recognition of the need to include men (husbands) in maternal and child health programmes in view of their existing and potential role in promoting egalitarian decisions about reproductive and maternal health as partners/ husbands, fathers and community members. Despite strong recommendation of the World Health Organization to ensure husband participation in maternal and child healthcare, there is dearth of evidence based research on this topic.

It is quite heartening to note that Dr. Gyanvati has conducted empirical research on this much needed and highly relevant theme. Her study gives an insight into the involvement of the husband during pregnancy and lactating stages of the wife and its implications on the health and well-being of the mother and child. A comparative analysis of the two locales - rural areas and urban slums of Delhi - form the central aspect of the study. It gives a deeper understanding on the usage of maternal healthcare services, influencing extrinsic and intrinsic factors and their influence on women as critical variables in the study. Major research trends and theoretical underpinnings are highlighted. Exhaustive literature review is done and gaps are appropriately presented.

A well defined research methodology with clear objectives has been laid down for the study. Elaborate conceptual framework on maternal health, husband's involvement in maternal healthcare and barriers affecting husbands' participation is delineated.

In the book, the author has very aptly and efficiently analyzed the linkage between maternal healthcare service utilization and socio-demographic variables like age of women, age at marriage, educational levels, type of family, occupation, etc. In addition, details covering variables like intra-extra familial factors affecting usage of pregnancy services, child health data, milestone development of children, factors affecting utilization of services, views of husband participation in maternal healthcare in terms of physical, economic, information support, communication between couples, decision-making, are presented with statistical dexterity. Major facilitative and inhibitive factors in husband participation have been beautifully depicted in the chapters.

The book, consisting of five chapters, is highly relevant for social work and public healthcare educators, practitioners and scholars as well as policy makers. The author deserves congratulations for successfully making existing pool of public health and social work knowledge more richer and offering efficient model of interventions for ensuring improved husband participation in maternal and child healthcare.

Archana Kaushik
Associate Professor
University of Delhi
Delhi

Preface & Acknowledgements

Husband-participation in maternal healthcare is very relevant in the current scenario. In Cairo in 1994, the International Conference on Population and Development for the first time highlighted the significance of husband-participation or husband involvement in motherhood and women's reproductive health. Maternal health is one essential component of women's reproductive health. Maternal healthcare is one of the Millennium Development Goals (Goal -5). In addition, 'Ensure healthy lives and promote well-being for all ages' is one of the Sustainable Development Goals (SDG-3); reduction of the global maternal mortality ratio to less than 70 deaths/per one lakh live births by 2030 is being targeted. The Maternal Mortality Rate (MMR) is 130 deaths per one lakh live births and infant mortality rate 34 deaths per one thousand live births in India (Registrar General of India, 2014-16). Husband-participation in maternal healthcare is an accepted and well-embraced phenomenon in the western countries.

In India, it is the first time that the National Population Policy (2000) has emphasized the increased participation of men in planned parenthood. Husband-participation in maternal healthcare of their wife is quite restricted in Indian society because pregnancy care is considered women's domain. But now the changed scenario dictates that the domain of pregnancy care is the responsibility of both partners. Husband-participation in maternal healthcare can be one of the preventive strategies to reduce maternal mortality rate (MMR) and infant mortality rate (IMR) in any country including India.

The purpose of writing this work is to provide perspectives, communicate and create positive behavior related to husband-participation in maternal healthcare that would lead to healthy mothers and their newborn infants. The book is divided into five chapters. Chapter 1 introduces the topic of husband-participation in maternal healthcare. Chapter 2 focuses on utilization of maternal healthcare services in rural and slum areas. Chapter

3 reflects on the husband – a critical actor in maternal healthcare services. Chapter 4 presents marital relation and utilization of maternal healthcare services. The last chapter deals with social work intervention and presents a conclusion. This book also contains case studies related to participation and non-participation of husband in maternal healthcare.

I hope that this book will be quite helpful for students, policy makers and academicians of social sciences along with practitioners and educators in the field of public health, family studies and developmental studies.Like others, my research work also carries the footprint, contribution and impact of many individuals, groups and institutions. Firstly I would like to express my deep gratitude to my guide, Dr. Archana Kaushik for her unstinting help, support, and guidance during all the stages of the present research work. Her patience, depth of understanding of the subject and loving insistence on perfecting minor details helped me to enjoy research work.

I would like to thank Prof. Neera Agnimitra, Head of the Department and Prof. Sanjay Bhatt, Ph.D. Coordinator, for their timely advice and encouragement.

I owe my gratitude to the entire faculty of the Department of Social Work, University of Delhi, for their sustained encouragement.

I would like to specially thank Prof. Mohan Raju, Department of Education, University of Delhi for his help and advice in statistical analysis.

My special thanks goes to all the respondents for giving me their valuable time for collecting necessary data with respect to the present work. Their support and cooperation was valuable, given their preoccupation with their household work, jobs and so on.

I am also thankful to Department of Women and Child Development, Government of Delhi, District ASHA Coordinators, ASHA workers, ANMs and *Anganwadi* workers for extending all possible help and support for locating the respondents.

My friend Ms. Eshita Sharma deserves a special mention for helping in locating library resources.

Further, I would also like to thank my parents for their continuous support and encouragement in fulfilling my dream. In fact, their contribution can never be expressed fully in words. I am also grateful to my brothers, Kapil and Vivek and sister Sheetal for their incessant support.

I thank the publishing house for highest quality of publication.

Lastly, I would like to thank God for showering blessings and courage on me to complete this small journey of finding what I am capable of doing and trusting myself.

Chapter – 1

Husband-Participation in Maternal Healthcare: An Introduction

Maternal health is related to the Right to Health of women. Access to adequate facilities during pregnancy and childbirth is an important component. Qualit y healthcare in these stages is the right of both the woman and the unborn child. Maternal Health was among one of the Millennium Development Goals (MDG-5); to improve health of mothers and reduce the maternal mortality to 109 death/per one lakh live births by 2015 was being targeted. 'Ensure healthy lives and promote well- being for all ages' is one of the Sustainable Development Goals (SDG-3); to reduce the global maternal mortality ratio to less than 70 death/per one lakh live births by 2030 is being targeted (United Nation Development Programme, 2015). However, the current situation of maternal health in the country is abysmal and needs urgent attention. The Maternal Mortality Rate (MMR) is 167 deaths per one lakh live births in India (Sample Registration System, 2011-13). Every year, 45,000 women in the country die from pregnancy-related complications, which is more than in any other country (WHO, 2015).

The state of maternal health in the country can improve significantly if pregnant women get quality care with regard to three stages of services such as the Ante Natal Care (ANC), Natal care (NC) and Post Natal Care (PNC), which would help to identify pregnancy risks and minimize them. Better maternal healthcare services directly lead to the delivery and care of a healthy newborn, thereby reducing the rate of infant mortality rate (IMR) as well as maternal mortality rate (MMR).

Health is a most fundamental aspect of human well-being. It has evolved over the centuries as a concept from an individual concern to a world-wide social goal and encompasses the whole quality of life. Health is a multifactorial or multi-dimensional phenomena. The factors that influence health lie both within the individual and externally in the society in which he or she lives. It is true to say that what an individual is and to what diseases he/she may fall victim depends on a combination of two sets of factors – his/her genetic factors and the environmental factors to which he/she is exposed. These factors interact and these interactions influence health- promotion. Thus, conceptually, the health of individuals and whole communities may be considered to be the result of many interactions (Park, 2002 & 2009).

There are many factors that influence health in general as well as maternal health in particular. These variables are socio-cultural (such as gender bias, early marriage, etc.), economic (like poverty, malnutrition, etc.), political (such as low quality of services, unfriendly behavior of hospital staff, etc.) and environmental (continued physical work, heavy workload, etc.), apart from participation of husbands in maternal healthcare.

In general, it is maintained that women in rural villages remain unaware about the significance of maternal healthcare services for them. Often they are dependent on elder members of the family for availing maternal healthcare services. There are various factors such as cultural and traditional practices related to pregnancy of women that affect usage of services. Generally, women in rural areas have to get involved in household and agricultural work.

According to Urban Resource Centre (2007), rural village in Delhi is defined as follows: "these are villages that exist within the Delhi but are yet to be notified as urban villages. Often these tend to be on the periphery of the city". According to National Family Health Survey–III (NFHS-III), 52.9% of deliveries are at home in rural areas of Delhi (2005-06). Study by Sagar (2006) mentioned that 27.5% women in rural areas delivered in the hospital in the care of the doctor and nurse.

The process of urbanization has led to an increase in the number of slum communities with lack of basic civic facilities. People residing in slum areas are invariably migrants from other states and they face a number of problems such as job insecurity, poverty, unhygienic conditions, restricted accessibility to maternal healthcare services and so on. In Slum Area Improvement and Clearance Act, 1956, (section-3) "slums have been defined as mainly those residential areas where dwellings are in any respect unfit for human habitation by reasons of dilapidation, overcrowding, faulty designs of buildings, narrowness or faulty arrangement of streets, lack of ventilation, light or sanitation facilities or any combination of these factors which are detrimental to safety, health and morals" (Ministry of Home Affairs, 2011). Women have poor maternal health care services due to lack of health facilities, lack of visits conducted by the ANMs and other health staff members in slum areas. In general, women in slums remain unaware of maternal healthcare services. These are various factors that lead to poor utilization of maternal healthcare services and hence childbirth often takes place at home. The two studies conducted in Delhi and Mumbai reveal that socio-economic condition is a major factor that influences use of maternal healthcare services by women in slum areas (Agarwal, Singh & Garg, 2007 & Sarode, 2007).Another study by Khan, Mehnaz, Ansari, Khalique and Siddiqui, (2009) conducted in two slums of Aligarh city, shows that major barriers for low utilization of maternal healthcare services by women in slum are traditional, financial and the rude behavior of health staff.

Women, in a patriarchal social structure like India, are often considered vulnerable. There are multifarious dimensions of this gender based vulnerability – since ancient and medieval times, women have been discouraged to acquire education and access other developmental avenues. Their roles are confined mainly to the four walls of the household. Kakkar (1982) maintains that age and sex have been two guiding principles in defining family relationships — males have more authority than females and elders enjoy greater respect and control than youngsters. The implications of such norms are visible even today in many families. Mothers-in-law have been considered to be the prime decision-makers in matters related to maternal and child care. In patriarchal structures of Indian society, women have been often found caught up in multiple and repeated pregnancies that take a heavy toll on their health and life (Ganesh, 1997). Women, more or less, remain passive on decisions related to antenatal care, natal care, postnatal care and child care (see: Ganesh, 1997; Jamuna, 1995 & Kakkar, 1982). Are these family dynamics still powerful in the contemporary world?

Husband Participation in Maternal Healthcare

Husband's participation in the maternal healthcare of women is very essential to ensure a healthy mother and child. It may be one of the preventable strategies for maternal deaths in India. In traditional societies, generally, men or husbands have been uninformed about the pregnancy concerns of the wife. And maternal health is always considered the women's domain in the Indian society. Men have traditionally remained uninformed about their wife's pregnancy-related experiences and needs, yet are significant decision-makers with regard to pregnancy–related care and expenditure (Jejeebhoy & Varkey, 2004).

Attention to men's involvement in reproductive health received an impetus following the Programme of Action forged in 1994, at the International Conference on Population and Development (ICPD) (Cairo

Programme of Action, September 1994). Under the Programme, focus was on men playing a key role to promote gender equality and encouraging and enabling men to take responsibility for their sexual andreproductive behavior and their social and family roles (Chapter-4 Gender equalit y and empowerment of women, ICPD, 1994). The Programme also highlights women's health and safe motherhood, placing emphasis on education to engage men's support for maternal health and safe motherhood; all countries are urged to seek changes in high-risk sexual behavior and to devise strategies to ensure that men share responsibility for sexual and reproductive health (Chapter-8 Health, Morbidity and Mortality, ICPD, 1994).

There is a need to develop ways and means to implement the ICPD+5 recommendation, which urges Governments and their partners to "support public health education to create awareness of the risks of pregnancy, labour and delivery and to increase the understanding of the respective roles and responsibilities of family members, including men, as well as of civil society and Governments, in promoting and protecting maternal health" (United Nations, 1999).

The article written by Maharaj (2000) focuses on the important fact that male support is necessary for women to progress safely through pregnancy and child birth, and to provide couples with the best opportunity of having a healthy child. Male decisions impact women's health quite significantly. Men have an important role to play in ensuring that their pregnant partner receives proper care during and after pregnancy. Every year, millions of women get pregnant and many of these pregnancies areunintended. Sometimes pregnancy-related complications lead to death.

Added to this, Kumar and Singh, (n.d.) analyze individual (such as age, education, exposure to mass media, working status, age-gap and educational gap between husband and wife), household (including religion, wealth index, household structure, caste/tribe) and contextual factors (like region, urban-rural place of residence, wife-beating and attitude towards wife's sexual rights) affecting male involvement in the maternal health of their wives in India using data from National Family Health Survey, 2005-06. The study also reveals that over half of such men accompanied their wife for ANC when they were pregnant with their youngest child. Increasing educational gap between husband and wife adversely affects the male participation in maternal health.

Husband's involvement in maternal healthcare of women is helpful in terms of providing better health care and to ensure the institutional delivery of pregnant women. The health system and health professionals are seeing the need to increase couple counseling about maternal healthcare and to educate the husband about each and every aspect of maternal healthcare. It may be helpful to realize that husband participation ensures better health and care of mother and new born child. So, in the contemporary world, it is important to note that maternal healthcare is not the domain of women only, but it is a joint effort of both husband and wife.

Concept of Husband-Participation

Male involvement

Men's involvement in pregnancy care has been emphasized in different studies identifying the sectors where men can contribute towards the well-being of their pregnant wives (Drennan, 1998).

'Male involvement' is used as an umbrella term to encompass the various ways in which men relate to reproductive health problems and programs, reproductive rights and reproductive behavior. Male involvement in reproductive health has two major facets:-

(i) The way men accept and indicate support towards their partners' needs, choices and rights in reproductive health; and

(ii) Men's own reproductive and sexual behavior (Kumar, 1996).

Male participation

Kumar (1996) defines the term participation, referring to men's supportive role in their families, communities, and work place to promote gender equity, girls' education, women's empowerment and sharing of household chores and child-rearing. The study also suggests a more active role of men in both decision-making and behaviors such as sharing their reproductive decision with their partners, supporting their partner's choices and using contraception and /or periodic abstinence.

Men as partners

Men need to share some of the responsibilities of household work and parenting, thereby reducing the burden on women. It also focuses on ensuring equitable and need-based distribution of resources among men/ boys and women/girls. They need tosupport women to seek healthcare by giving monetary resources. They are also required to show empathy and understanding during ill-health, accompany women to the health centers and acting as enablers for the women to implement their decisions (Khanna, Kapadia & Dongre, 1998).

According to Dutta (2002), in safe motherhood and child development, men can play key roles such as –

1. Antenatal care (ANC)
    - Helping pregnant women to stay healthy

- Making sure that she gets proper ANC by providing money for transportation to pay for her visits
- Accompanying her to ANC visits and learning about the symptoms of pregnancy complication
- Ensuring that she receives nutritious food

2. Natal care services (delivery)
   - Arranging for skilled care during delivery
   - By paying for services
   - Arranging transportation and other requirements in case of emergency
3. Avoiding delays in seeking care. There are three types of delays that put a mother's health at risk
   - Delay in deciding to seek care
   - Delay in getting to healthcare facility
   - Delay in receiving adequate care at the facilities
4. Post natal care: - helping after the birth of new born child
   - Making sure that woman gets nutritious food
   - Helping women by doing heavy household work
   - Encouraging breast-feeding
   - Using contraceptives

There are numerous ways in which men influence women's health. Men or husbands'- participation can have a positive effect on women's health by:

- Using or supporting the use of contraception so that sexual partners are able to control the number and timing of pregnancies.
- Encouraging women to have adequate nutrition during pregnancy and providing physical, financial, and emotional support.
- Supporting women during pregnancy, delivery, and the postpartum period.
- Supporting the physical and emotional needs of post-abortion women.
- Preventing all forms of violence against women.
- Working to end harmful traditional practices such as female genital mutilation (Padma, 2005).

Conceptual Framework

The World Health Organization (1948) defines Health as a state of complete physical, mental and social well-being and not merely the absence of disease or infirmity. Later "the ability to lead a socially and economically productive life" was also included in the definition in 1978.

The World Health Organization (WHO) defines maternal health as the health of women during pregnancy, childbirth and the postpartum period. While motherhood is often a positive and fulfilling experience, for many women it is associated with suffering, ill-health and even death. The WHO (2000) states "pregnancy health is physical, mental and social wellbeing of women immediately before (antenatal), during pregnancy/delivery (natal) and after childbirth (post natal)".

Three stages of maternal healthcare

Ante-natal care (pre-natal care):- Ante-natal care is the care of women during pregnancy. The primary aim of antenatal care is to achieve, at the end of a pregnancy, a healthy mother and a healthy baby. In some countries, notification of pregnancy is required to bring the mother in the prevention care cycle as early as possible. Ideally, this care should begin soon after conception and continue throughout pregnancy. The objectives of ante – natal care are:

(i) To promote, protect and maintain the health of the mother during pregnancy;

(ii) To detect high risk cases and give them special attention;

(iii) To foresee complications and prevent them

(iv) To teach the mother elements of child care, nutrition, personal hygiene and environmental sanitation.

(v) To remove anxiety and dread associated with delivery. vi. To reduce maternal and infant mortality and morbidity.

(vii) To sensitize the mother to the need for family planning, including advice to cases seeking medical termination of pregnancy.

(viii) To attend to the under-fives accompanying the mother.

Intranatal care: Intranatal care means care during child birth. Child birth is a normal physiological process but complications may arise due to several reasons. Efficient natal care is very important even if the delivery is likely to be normal. The aims of natal care are:

(i) Thorough asepsis, delivery with minimum injury to the infant and the mother.

(ii) Preparedness to deal with any possible complications such as prolonged labour, mal-presentations.

(iii) Care of the baby at delivery, care of the eyes, etc.

Postnatal care: - Postnatal care is the care of the mother (and the new-born) after delivery. Broadly, this care falls into two areas: care of mother which primarily is the responsibility of the obstetrician; and care of the newborn. The objectives of postnatal care are:

(i) To provide care for the rapid restoration of the mother to optimum health.

(ii) To prevent the complications of the post-natal period.

(iii) To promote adequate breast feeding.

(iv) To provide basic health education to the mother and family.

(v) To provide family planning services (Park, 2002; Chowdhary, 1995).

Maternal Healthcare Indicators

(i) Percentage of mothers who had at least 3 antenatal care visits for their last birth.

(ii) Percentage of mothers who consumed IFA (Iron Folic Acid) for 90 days or more when they were pregnant with their last child.

(iii) Percentage of births assisted by doctor/nurse/LHV (lady health visitors)/ANM (Auxiliary Nurse Midwife)/other health personnel.

(iv) Percentage of institutional births.

(v) Percentage of mothers who received postnatal care from doctor/nurse/LHV/ANM/other health personnel within 2 days of delivery for their last birth (National Family Health Survey- III, 2005-06).

International Perspective on Safe Motherhood or Maternal Healthcare

The table below (table no. 1.01) shows that international organizations have highlighted the importance of maternal healthcare. These are discussed below:

The above table shows that international programs give emphasis on implementation of various programs related to safe motherhood or maternal healthcare of women. There is a linkage between healthy mothers and their healthy new born child and it helps to reduce the maternal and infant mortality rate in the world. It also emphasizes on equal accessibility of healthcare services to achieve ideal maternal healthcare.

National Perspective on Safe Motherhood or Maternal Healthcare

The table (table no. 1.02) shows that various documents or programs give importance to maternal healthcare of women in India. Those are discussed below:

Table No. 1.01 International Perspective on Safe Motherhood

International Declaration	***Importance on safe motherhood***
World Health Organization (1994)	Safe motherhood aims at attaining optimal maternal and newborn health. It implies reduction of maternal mortality and morbidity and enhancement of the health of newborn infants through equitable access to primary healthcare including family planning, prenatal, delivery and postnatal care for the mother and infant and access to essential obstetric and neonatal care.
The Rio Conference	Paragraphs 24.3 (e) and 6.26 of Agenda 21 call on government to implement programs that fully support women's productive and reproductive roles and well-being, with special attention to need for providing equal and improved healthcare for all children and the need to reduce the risk of maternal and child mortality and sickness.
The Vienna Conference	The importance of the enjoyment by women of highest standard of physical and mental health throughout their life-span and reducing infant and maternal mortality rates. The Programme of Action supports national and international cooperation in ensuring "safe maternity".
The Cairo Conference (1994)	Paragraph 8.19 states 'safe motherhood has been accepted in many countries as a strategy to reduce maternal morbidity and mortality".
The Copenhagen summit	6(p) of the Copenhagen Declaration commits government to "attain the maternal and child health objectives of Rio and Cairo.
The Beijing conference	The right of access to appropriate health-care services that will enable women to go safely through pregnancy and child birth and stresses prevention of unsafe abortion through adequate healthcare services, including family planning and emergency obstetric services.
Millennium Development Goals (MDG) 5	To improve health of mothers and reduce the maternal mortality to 109 deaths/per one lakh live births by 2015 was targeted.
Sustainable Development	To reduce the global maternal mortality ratio to less than 70
Goal (SDG) 3	death/per one lakh live births by 2030.

Source:- Boland, 1997; Promoting Reproductive Rights: A Global Mandate.

Table No. 1.02National declarations Importance of safe motherhood

Fifth Five-Year Plan (1974-79)	Maternal, child health and nutrition programs were integrated with family planning (Jejeebhoy &Varkey,2004).
Child Survival and Safe Motherhood Programme (1992)	It combined maternal and child health interventions. The key strategies focus on pregnancy related care and neo- natal care. They include first referral units, immunization, training ANMs and traditional birth attendants, etc. (Jejeebhoy &Varkey, 2004).
I Reproductive and Child Health Programme (1997-98)	It strategizes to enhance maternal and newborn health in four broad areas such as strengthening facilities and upgrading the skills of a variety of providers, institutional delivery and mobilizing community support, promoting skilled attendance at home and sub centre level, and advocating post partum and essential newborn care (Ministry of Health and Family Welfare, 2003).
II Reproductive and Child HealthProgramme (2005)	The objectives of maternal health under the RCH-II are • Improve access to skilled care and emergency obstetric care • Improve coverage and quality of antenatal care • Increase coverage of post-partum care (RCH-II, 2005).
National Rural Health Mission(2005)	The objective of the Mission is reducing maternal and neonatal mortality by promoting institutional delivery among the poor pregnant women (Ministry of Health and Family Welfare, 2006).
Janani Suraksha Yojana (JSY) (April, 2005)	To have incentive-based safe and institutional delivery of preg nant women (Ministry of Health and Family Welfare,2015-2016).
Indira Gandhi Matritva Sahyog Yojana (IGMSY) - A Conditional Maternity Benefit Scheme (2010)	To improve the health and nutrition status of pregnant and lactating women and infants by: Promoting appropriate practices, care and service utilization during pregnancy, safe delivery and lactation; Encouraging the women to follow (optimal) IYCF (Infant and Young Child Feeding) practicesincluding early and exclusive breast feeding for the first six months; Contributing to better enabling environment by providing cash incentives (Rs. 4000/-) for improved health and nutrition to pregnant and lactating mothers. Eligibility criteria: Pregnant women above 19 years. Husband is not working in government sector (Ministry of Women and Child Development, 2010).
Janani Shishu Suraksha Karyakram (JSSK) (1st June, 2011)	The initiative entitles all pregnant women delivering in public health institutions to free and no-expense delivery, including Caesarean Section (C-Section). To provide free drugs and consumables, free diet during stay for normal delivery and C-section, free diagnostics and free blood. To provide for free transport from home to institution, and between facilities in case of a referral and drop back home. To provide similar services for sick infants up to 1 year of age (Ministry of Health and Family Welfare, 2015-2016).
National Ambulance Services	To dial 102 services essentially consist of basic patient transport aimed to cater to the needs of pregnant women and children, though other categories are not excluded and are benefiting. This service can be accessed through a toll free call to a Call Centre (Ministry of Health and Family Welfare, 2015-2016).

Mother and Child TrackingSystem (MCTS)	To capture information and track all pregnant women and children (0-5 Years) so that they receive 'full' maternal and child health services (Ministry of Health and Family Welfare, 2015-2016).
Mission *Indradhanush* (MI) (2014)	To reach 90 lakh unimmunized/partially immunized children by 2020 (Ministry of Health and Family Welfare, 2015-2016).
Kilkari & Mobile Academy (2016)	To create proper awareness among pregnant women, parents of children and field workers about the importance of Ante Natal Care (ANC), Institutional Delivery, Post-Natal Care (PNC) and Immunization. In the first phase Kilkari would be launched in 6 States viz. Uttarakhand, Jharkhand, Uttar Pradesh,Odisha, Rajasthan (HPDs- High Priority Districts) and Madhya Pradesh (HPDs- High Priority Districts). The Mobile Academy would be launched in 4 States viz. Uttarakhand, Jharkhand, Rajasthan and Madhya Pradesh. Mobile Academy is an anytime, anywhere audiotraining course on inter-personal communication skills that the ASHA/ANM can access from her mobile phone. It gives ASHAs tips on how to convince families to adopt priority RMNCH (Reproductive, Maternal, Newborn Child Health) behaviors, while refreshing her existing knowledge. Also these services will be free of cost to States/UTs and the beneficiaries (Ministry of Health and Family Welfare, 2015-2016).
MAA (Mothers' Absolute Affection) Programme(2016)	To revitalize efforts towards promotion, protection and sup port of breastfeeding practices through health systems in order to achieve higher breastfeeding rates.The following are the objectives of the Programme in orderto achieve the above mentioned goal: Build an enabling environment for breastfeedingthrough awareness-generation activities, targeting pregnant and lactating mothers, family members and society in order to promote optimal breastfeeding practices. Breastfeeding to be positioned as an important intervention for child survival and development. Reinforce lactation support services at public health facilities through trained healthcare providers and through skilled community health workers. To incentivize and recognize those health facilities that show high rates of breastfeeding along with processes in place for lactation management (Ministry of Health and Family Welfare, 2016).
Pradhan Mantri Surakshit Matritva Abhiyan (2016)	The program aims to provide assured, comprehensive and quality antenatal care, free of cost, universally to all pregnant women on the 9th of every month. Works towards motivating private practitioners to volunteer for the campaign developing strategies for generating awareness, and appealing to the private sector to participate in the Abhiyan at government health facilities (Ministry of Health and Family Welfare, 2015-2016).
Pregnancy Aid Yojana (2016)	Under maternity benefit scheme Rs. 6000/- each will be transferred directly to the bank account of pregnant women who undergo institutional delivery and immunization of their child (Union Budget, 2017-2018).

The above table (no.1.02) reflects that various documents give significance to maternal and child health in India. These programs also focus to provide appropriate training for untrained or traditional *dais* in case a pregnant woman is not able to reach the hospital for delivery. Integrating the traditional *dais* in the programs may be effective strategies for ensuring the safe delivery of pregnant women. On the other hand, these programs also focus on interpersonal communication, cash-based incentives, breast feeding practice, etc. to promote the health of mothers and their newborn children. It may be noted that the government has proposed estimated budget for health as Rs. 47,352.51 crore, in the recent Annual Budget session in which scheme of maternity assistance is Rs. 2,700 crore in 2017-2018 (TOI, 2017).

Factors or barriers affecting husband-participation in maternal healthcare

In India, generally husbands face various challenges and obstacles such as lack of information, low literacy, religion, couple relationship, job compulsion, violence, alcohol, cultural practices, gender role norms, women's domain, wives' unwillingness, distance, cost, lack of privacy, lack of space, harsh language use by staff members, timing of health centers, lack of communication by health personnel, etc., for non-participation in maternal healthcare for their wives. A study mentioned that the most prominent barriers to male involvement in maternal health of their wives included low levels of knowledge, patriarchal beliefs, shyness/ embarrassment and job constraints (Mullany, 2006; Carter & Speizer, 2005). Another study conducted in the rural area of Mwanza district in Southern Malawi, finds that two main reasons of barriers to husband involvement in maternal healthcare are gender role norms and unfriendly health system issues (Kululanga, Sundby, Chirwa,Malata & Maluwa, 2012; Sosten, Paul, Jack & Robert, 2015). The qualitative study by Secka (2010) conducted in Gambia, highlights that restriction of involvement of husband in pregnancy and child birth is due to socio-economic and cultural factors, husband's limited knowledge on danger signs, health service and structural factors. A qualitative study conducted in four rural hill villages in the Gorkha district of Nepal by Lewis, Lee and Simkhada (2015), identifies that the husband's role is shaped by various factors such as husband availability, cultural beliefs and traditions. The longitudinal study by Tinkew, Ryan, Carrano and Moore (2007) notes that husbands who did not want the pregnancy are less likely to exhibit paternal warmth following the birth. Further, the study by Vermeulen, Miltenburg, Barras, Maselle, Elteren and Roosmalen, reported that main barriers for husband non-participation in maternal healthcare are traditional gender roles, lack of knowledge, low accessibility to join antenatal care visits and previous negative experiences in health facilities in Magu district, rural Tanzania (2016).

The quasi-experimental study in Nepal finds that women with husbands present at deliver y time felt higher personal control during childbirth as compared to those women who were accompanied by female friends or received no support during childbirth (Sapkota, Kobayashi, Kakehashi, Baral & Yoshida, 2012).

Thus, the above discussion shows found that various factors influencing husband participation can be categorized as self, social, cultural practices, low economic status, behavior of health providers and health services. In patriarchal society, husbands or men are never encouraged to provide support to their wives during pregnancy, delivery and after-delivery care. At times, even if a husband wants to participate in maternal healthcare of his wife, these factors pose hindrance for him.

Husband's participation in wife's pregnancy period helps her stay healthy

Men's supportive participation or stance in pregnancy care of their wives can help in protecting the lives and health of women as they become mothers and attend to their children. The maternal mortality in India is second highest in the world (Razi, 2012). Most of the women who die or are severely injured in pregnancy or childbirth reside in sub-Saharan Africa and Asia, and most of the deaths are caused by hemorrhage, high blood pressure, unsafe abortion or sepsis- almost all of them preventable (UNICEF, 2012).Husband-participation in maternal healthcare has been found to have asignificant positive impact on women and their new born child's health. A study in India on providing antenatal education to men or fathers noted a significant impact with higher frequency of accompaniments for antenatal check-ups visits. It also highlighted that men or husbands who were aware of antenatal care education and about various methods of family planning, were more apprehended about their wife's nutritional intake needs during pregnancy (Raju & Leonard, 2000). A good amount of nutritional intake of foods and ensuring more rest are both important for women during pregnancy. Men or husbands' participation can help women have safe maternal healthcare by ensuring that they receive nutritious food intake such as food rich in iron and fortified with vitamin A. (Sharma & Desai, 1992; Sherpa & Rai, 1997; UNICEF, 1998 & AAWH, 1998). The UNDP (Human Development) report revealed that 88 percent of pregnant women (age 15-49 years) were suffering from anemia (Razi, 2012). Anemia, while not a direct cause of maternal deaths, is a factor in almost all such mortalities.

An anemic woman is five times more likely to die of pregnancy-related causes (Viterif, 1994).

Safe motherhood or maternal healthcare consists of ensuring good health for the woman and her new born child during antenatal care, natal care (delivery care), and the post- natal care (after the delivery care). The men or husbands' participation plays a key role in all three phases. Man's decisions and actions often make the difference between illness and health, life and death (AAWH, 1998; Sherpa & Rai, 1997 & Thaddeus & Maine, 1994). A review article states that benefits of husband-participation in maternal healthcare includes the following: increased use of family planning and contraceptives in long-term couples,; reduced workload for women, improved preparation of child birth, improved couple communication and emotional support, and increased attendance at postnatal care (Davis, Luchters & Holmes, 2013). Another study finds that women mentioned the reasons for husband-participation in maternal healthcare such as love and couple communication, concerns about mother and their child's health, wish to avoid complications, knowledge about pregnancy care, responsibility and obligation of husbands, ensuring proper utilization of pregnancy related services, arranging transport for institutional delivery, emotional support and understanding pain at time of childbirth (Carter, 2002). A qualitative study finds that women most frequently-mentioned types of support like practical help with routine activities, information/advice, emotional support and assurance, as well as the provision of resources and material goods from their mothers,mother-in-laws, husbands and sister-in-laws during the pregnancy in Matlab, Bangladesh (Edmonds, Paul & Sibley, 2011). Thus, husband-participation may ensure the better health of their wives and unborn child as well as prevent various complications during the pregnancy.

Participation in arranging for skilled care during delivery time period

Men or husband's participation may be helpful in terms of a supportive stance in ensuring an institutional delivery or a delivery attended by professional or trained personnel of their wives. There are only 42 % of births that are professionally supervised or attended in our country (Razi, 2012). In developing countries, most women give birth without skilled assistance, helped by untrained traditional attendants or by family members. It may be true that both husband and wife do not give much importance to birth by trained personnel and there may a ls o be a lack of availability of medical services. The survey by the Registrar General of India and Sample Registration System (2010) brings out that 25 % of deliveries are assisted by untrained functionaries in India (The Times of India, 2012). The presence of a trained or skilled attendant during childbirth can make a big difference in the life of pregnant women. Husband's participation can help by arranging and paying for a trained attendant to be present with their wives during the delivery. They also can arrange ahead of time for transport, buy supplies and fulfill other medical requirements.

Participation after the arrival of new born baby

Husbands' participation after the birth of new born baby is essential in terms of ensuring the availability of nutritional foods, child care, child immunization, breast feeding and adopting the family planning methods. In the post-natal care period, men or husbands have an important role to play in household work, such as fetching water and caring of other children. Finally, it is crucial for the couple to begin using family planning methods, either a temporary method to space the next birth or a vasectomy if no more children are desired (AAWH, 1998 & Sherpa & Rai, 1997). Husband-participation in family planning is essential for both the wife's health as well as overall well-being of family. Also husbands' participation may enable them to support their wives' choices and use various family planning methods. Men or husbands' participation may ensure that they accompany their wives for immunization of new born child, as well as take care of the new born child.

Husband-participation in family planning

Husband-participation or involvement is significant in adopting any family planning methods which ensure the better health of women and their children; it also helps in proper spacing between the children. This can be verified through various articles. The article written by Helzner (1996) focuses on the importance of male involvement in family planning and interplay between men's and women's role in the same. A study by Mihira, Nancy and Joyce (1997) brings out that male involvement in family planning decisions to decrease family size can motivate a process that results in long-term benefits for women, and male acceptance of family planning methods. A study by Odhiambo (1997) conducted in Kenya, shows that men are becoming more involved and supportive in family planning.

Implication of husband-participation in maternal healthcare on women's health

There are several experimental and intervention-based studies in Baroda by Deepak Charitable Trust (DCT) that highlight that husbands who are aware tend to be more involved in their wife's antenatal care and child birth. It also reveals that most men support the need for medical check-ups of their wife during pregnancy because it would be useful to detect complications early. Both men and women also agreed that men were responsible for ensuring antenatal care (Pelon, Rob & Khan, 1999). Another study conducted by Varkey, Huntington, Das et al. (2002) in Delhi, reveals that 80% of pregnant women and their husbands wanted husbands to participate in maternity care. Moreover, when permitted, 60% of their husbands attended antenatal clinics with their wives. The study also confirms that couple counseling in antenatal and postpartum period was positively associated with acceptance of family planning. The experimental study conducted in Nepal, finds that an antenatal health education intervention involving husbands increased postpartum care utilization among women compared with women who received antenatal health education alone and with women who received no education. In addition, women educated with their husbands were more likely to be highly prepared for birth compared with women receiving no education. Women educated with their husbands were more aware about pregnancy related complications and family planning methods after delivery as compared to the other two groups (Mullany, Becker & Hindin, 2006; 2007 & Mullany, Lakhey, Shrestha, Hindin & Becker, 2009). Further, study by Mullick, Kunene and Wanjiru (2005) find that all the groups were less likely to want their partners at delivery (66 percent control, 72 percent intervention) compared to other activities such as beingaccompanied to postpartum visits (94 percent control, 97 percent intervention). Men were generally in agreement with women in respect of clinic based activities, such as accompanying women to the clinic and postpartum visits.

Study Safe Motherhood Male Involvement Research Project (SMMI) in Morgan District in Nepal, states that husband support in reducing women's household work contributes to prevention of maternal ill health (Horstman, Nepal & Pant, 2004). A study by Mosunmola, Adekunbi and Foluso conducted in Ogun state in Nigeria, 86.5% of women mentioned that their husband's support made pregnancy less stressful for them, 94.5% cited that their husband's provision of their needs gave them emotional security and 83.5% understood that lack of husband's support during pregnancy, labor and delivery was dangerous (2014). The study by Story, Burgard, Lori, Taleb, Ali and Hoque (2012) finds that only those women get emotional, instrumental and informational support from their husbands who utilized institutional delivery care during delivery, as compared to those women whose delivery took place at home in rural sub- district of Netrokona district, Bangladesh. A review paper by Yargawa and Leonardi-Bee (2015) reveals that husband-involvement during pregnancy and at post-natal care appeared to have more benefits as compared to delivery time or childbirth. It also improved overall utilization of maternal healthcare services.

The Cross-sectional study by Wai, Shibanuma, Oo, Fillman and Jimba (2015) in Yangon, Myanmar, show that there is a direct relationship between use of maternal healthcare services by women and husbands accompanying them for antenatal check-ups and delivery. These above studies bring out that husband-participation or husband support in maternal healthcare has positive impact on both couples or partners and their newborn child in terms of proper use of maternal healthcare services, enhancing husbands' knowledge, preparation for complications, child health, child immunization, etc., and is most significant in preventing maternal mortality and infant mortality.

Paternity leave

In India, generally pregnancy care is considered women's domain. For working women, maternity leave of 26 weeks is provided during their maternal period. But, till recently, there were no such provisions for husbands or fathers for getting paid leave during and after pregnancy of their wives. Changing work culture and life style demands both husband and wife's involvement in pregnancy and child care. Various types of leaves such as maternity leave, parental leave and paternity leave related to pregnancy and after child birth are significant for the health of pregnant women and their new born child. It is also important to understand that both parents can positively contribute to the development and care of the newborn baby. Paternity leave for husband has become one of the mechanisms for ensuring husband-participation in maternal healthcare of their wife. Generally, it may ensure better maternal health outcome of women and their newborn child. According to the All India Services (Leave) rules (1955), section-18 (B) paternity leave has been defined as "*A male member of the service (including a probationer) with less than two surviving children, may be granted paternity leave by an authority competent to grant leave for a period of 15 days, during the confinement of his wife for childbirth, i.e. up to 15 days before, or up to six months from the date of delivery of the child*" apply to officers appointed under central government of India. Another Delhi Judicial Service (Leave) Rules, (2011), section-34 defines paternity leave as "*A male member of the service with less than two surviving children may be granted paternity leave by the Competent Authority for a period of 15 days during the confinement of his wife for childbirth" and this* applies to officers appointed to the Delhi Judicial Service. According to Human Impact Patterns Report (2011), parental leave provides better prenatal and postnatal care and also strengthens parental bonding. It also provides long-term benefits that improve a child's brain development, social development and overall well-being. According to the New Children and Families Bill (U.K.), 50 weeks leave for both father and mother has been granted, which they can share for child care (TOI, 2014).

Table no. 1.03 Significance of Husband-Participation in Maternal Healthcare

Maternal healthcare situation in India	*Husband–participation inmaternal care*
• MMR – 167/1,00000 • 5 women died every hour • 45,000 women died in a year • Institutional delivery-78.9% • IMR- 37/1000 (SRS,2015) • U5MR- 43/10000 • Underweight 35.7% and 58.4% (Anemic) among under five children	• Identification of pregnancy complications • Prevention of various health problems • Help in heavy household work • Less stressful and emotional support • Physical support • Proper/more use of pregnancy care, institutional delivery care

Sources: National Family Health Survey-IV, 2015-16; TOI, 2016; WHO, 2015; SRS 2015; & SRS, 2011-2013].

Thus, the above discussion highlights the importance of husband-participation in maternal healthcare of their wife. Husband participation is significant to the better health of women and their newborn child. This could also go a long way in preventing maternal and infant mortality.

Socio-cultural and economic dimensions

There are several socio-cultural factors such as strong preference for male child, inequitable allocation of resources such as food and healthcare, arranged marriage for very young girls, education and income and as well as gender bias that hamper maternal health (Development in Practice' 1996; Haider,1995). Another study in Jharkand by Rani, Ghosh and Sharan (2007) shows that the majority of women had married at a young age, i.e. 15 years, which itself is a major factor having negative implications on maternal health. Another reviewed study finds that marriage before 18 years among girls leads to more cases of miscarriage and still birth (Santhya, Ram, Acharya, Jejeebhoy, Ram & Singh, 2010).

Several studies show that a woman who wishes to obtain healthcare, whether from a local traditional practitioner, the district hospital, or some intermediate provider, is not free to do so on her own. She must obtain permission from her husband or in-laws, be accompanied by a male family member if she travels outside the village, and somehow arrange money to pay for services, medicines, or for conveyance even if the care itself was free (Development in practice', 1996; Barua, Pande, Macquarrie & Walia, 2004). Gupta (1996) finds that one of the important reasons for survival of the traditional system of medicine is the economic poverty of people.

A study by Pathak, Pandey and Ojha (2001) focuses on Tamil Nadu, Madhya Pradesh and Orissa. It finds that there is a strong positive relationship between the utilization of ANC services and the socio-economic background of mother in terms of literacy, place of residence and the standard of living. The use of ANC services motivates pregnant women to deliver in hospital or at home under the supervision of a professional. Another studyattempting to investigate the utilization of ANC services in three states (Jharkhand, Chhattisgarh and Uttaranchal) by Pandey, Roy, Sahu and Acharya (2004) shows that women living in urban areas are more likely to go for ANC services compared with rural areas. Delivery care in the three smaller states varied with the socio-economic characteristics of its population. A further study by Padma (2005) states that every three out of four women had undergone the necessary tests for identifying a risky pregnancy in Andhra Pradesh. Women from lower socio-economic status still prefer to have a delivery at home with the help of *dai*. The types of care given during the post-partum period generally related to food intake, that too in the form of restriction on diet.

The economic status is another factor that affects the usage of maternal healthcare services among the pregnant women. Women belonging to low economic status resort to childbirth at home and they often have inadequate nutritional food intake during pregnancy and after childbirth. Why do women prefer delivery at home when government is making efforts to provide free of cost health facilities for pregnant women?

Public Services

Several studies reveal that there is limited availability of quality services, poor quality of care for women, unfriendly behavior of some of the governmental staff. Also, many grassroots level healthcare providers were not even sure what services should be provided after delivery and unreasonably high levels of fees were being charged by private centers. These are the factors that lead to not availing antenatal services, and antenatal care remains poor as majority of deliveries take place at home. Although both blocks (Chas & Chandankiari blocks in Bokaro district of Jharkhand) have primary health centers, few deliveries are conducted in these facilities. Assessing referral hospitals is difficult as most villages are connected only by mud roads. Lack of transportation, or the health facility is situated too far, a wide urban-rural differential, lack of knowledge, some villages being completely isolated are listed as the major reasons for not visiting the government health facilities (Bawa, 2003; Jejeebhoy & Varkey, 2004; Padma, 2005; Manju, 2006; Barnes, 2007 & Nagdeve, 2008).

An article by Kausar (2005) highlights that the extent of maternal mortality is an indicator of disparity and inequity in access to appropriate healthcare and nutrition services throughout a lifetime, and particularly during pregnancy and childbirth.The study by Hazarika finds that wealth is one of the strongest determinants of use of skilled birth attendants, with the poor being at a disadvantage. There are significant differences in the use of skilled delivery care among the urban and rural populations in India. Women in urban areas are more likely to use skilled attendants. Muslim women and women with lower levels of education are also less likely to avail skilled delivery services. The use of skilled care depended significantly on the place of delivery. Women who gave history of antenatal visits were more likely to have skilled attendants at birth. The researcher's analysis demonstrates that there are several financial, social, regional and cultural barriers to skilled birth attendant use in India (2010).

Public service is a major aspect which influences availability and accessibility of healthcare services or health set-ups for pregnant women. Generally, Government has made various provisions and free of cost services for pregnant women and newborns. However, reach and coverage of these programs and services are quite inadequate, and quality of healthcare is far from satisfactory. Maternal healthcare services are inaccessible due to various reasons such as locale disparity, rude behavior of health practitioners, lack of transportation facilities, long distant health settings and so on.

Environmental Dimension

Environment is another important factor that influences maternal healthcare of women. It covers variables like heavy household work done by pregnant women, lack of rest, lack of time for intake of nutritional food, etc., that impact maternal healthcare with outcomes like premature child birth, low birth weight of child, still birth, and so on. Haider (1995) states that nutrition and healthcare are affected by the amount of time available to women. And time is a scarce resource for women. Women working for long hours, engaged in heavy work that require energy-intensive, low-technology work, women with large household size, unmet nutritional and medical care needs affect maternal health. Further, Development in Practice, (1996) has mentioned that "continued physical activity until late pregnancy and a lack of adequate rest not only negatively affect women's health but also contributes to excessive rate of stillbirth, premature births, and intrauterine growth retardation".

Another study by Horstman, Nepal and Pant conducted in Morang District of Nepal revealed that 57 percent of pregnant women have worked as usual and 6 percent of them have more than usual. On the other hand, 49 percent of the women have worked inagriculture/daily wage work up to delivery and 23 percent of them ended this work more than six weeks before delivery (2004).

A study by Radkar and Parasuraman (2007) finds that large numbers of women need to fetch water from outside and need to go to the toilet; excessive physical activity is a precipitating factor for maternal mortality especially when the women's nutritional status is poor.

In India, generally it is a myth that women who do more household work and other work without rest have normal deliveries.

Husband-Participation in Maternal Healthcare

Husband-participation in maternal healthcare includes advising pregnant wife on her care, physical support, providing financial provisions and economic support, helping in heavy household work, etc. In general, when it comes to Indian men, it is often believed that due to inculcation of norms of masculinity, they have difficulty in doing tasks like providing emotional support to wife, communication or sharing feelings with her, help in managing crying children, changing nappies, cleaning clothes, cooking and so on during pregnancy, delivery and after delivery. A study by Block, Norr, Meyering, Norr and Charles (1981) reveals that husbands who have already had one child and who help their wives at home more also give more active support during delivery. The qualitative research study by Ross, Church, Hill, Seaman and Roberts conducted in Scotland with young men (16 to 25 years) and their teenage partners, finds that most of the young men were deeply involved in providing support and care to their partner during pregnancy, childbirth and after delivery (2012). Barua (1998) in Maharashtra shows that husbands also ignored women's health care during pregnancy, except for providing awareness on the need for antenatal registration and a nutritious diet. Men did advise their wives to reduce their workload during pregnancy; however, they themselves did not do anything to lighten the wife's burden, except in the case of nuclear families where husbands reported taking on more household tasks. In a qualitative study conducted in Kailali district of Nepal, respondents revealed that supportive role of husbands is largely in the form of giving advice, making financial arrangements and help in household work (Thapa, 2012).

The study conducted by Dutta (2002) finds that 43.5% of the husbands were not involved in any of the activities of antenatal care. The rest 56.5% were involved in at least one ofthe activities. It also revealed that 39% of husbands were not involved in any activity during labor or delivery. Only 16% husbands accompanied their wives to hospital. It also finds that 40.7% husbands did ensure rest for their wives after delivery or postnatal care.

A study by Pradhan, Khanna, Kukade and Ubale (2004) mentions that seven out of 42 men reported that they were asked by their wives to accompany them to the hospital. One third (14) of the 42 felt that they should have been involved in the consultation process. Only one man had talked to doctors. A study by Singh and Arora (2008) reveals that only in 14 (39%) cases, husbands accompany their wives to the doctor/hospital for antenatal visits. In ten cases, husband took time off work during their wives' pregnancy. Another study by Bhatta (2013) shows that 39.3% of husbands accompanied their wives for antenatal check- ups, 47.9% of husbands arranged for skilled birth attendants and 10.9% accompanied them for child immunization in Kathmandu. A study by Carter (2002) reveals that husbands are often involved in all three aspects of maternal health: pregnancy, birth and the postpartum period. The most common forms of husband involvement seemed to be giving money to women during pregnancy for prenatal care and helping out at home during the postpartum period. Another study by Mullany, Hindin and Becker (2005) finds that women attending ANC at a large urban hospital were accompanied by their husbands (40%) and reported that their husbands discussed health with them (75.0%), helped them in reducing their workload (57%), or helped to arrange birth plans with them (74%). The study by Iliyasu, Abubakar, Galadanci and Aliyu (2010) finds that 32.1% of husband accompanied their wives for maternal healthcare services and showed very little preparation for skilled assistance during delivery (6.2%), had savings for emergencies (19.5%) and arranged transportation during delivery (24.2%) in Ungogo, a Northern Nigerian Community. The study by Carter and Speizer (2005) show that overall 34% fathers participated in all three of the activities such as prenatal care visit, attended the delivery, or participated in a postpartum well-baby care visit. A study conducted in Addis Ababa of Ethiopia by Mekonnen (2009), shows that husbands provide support such as external tasks of health set-ups (for example pay bills) and help in household work (for example cooking) during prenatal term of their wives. It also highlights that modern healthcare set-up is a shared domain with both husband and wife involved in prenatal care.

Several studies reveal that husband awareness and knowledge about maternal healthcare services of their wife play important role in ensuring their involvement and better health of pregnant wife (Raju, 1999; Barua, Pande, Macquarrie & Walia, 2004 & Srivastava, 2011).Another study revealed that only fewer men recognized the dangers signs such as bleeding, swelling of face/hands, fever, long labor, etc., during pregnancy and childbirth (Singh, Bloom & Tusi, 1998 & Moore, 1999).

A study by Kululanga, Sundby, Malata and Chirwa conducted in rural and urban settings of Malawi, reveals that it is possible to encourage participation of men in maternal healthcare by using four main strategies, which are healthcare provider initiative, partner notification, couple initiative and community mobilization (2011). Another study conducted in urban slums of district Agra, states that 18.33% of husbands accompanied their wives during antenatal check-ups, 32.5% of husbands helped in household work, 67.5% of women did not receive help from their husbands and 87.5% of husbands were present during delivery (Awasthi, Nandan, Mahrotra & Shankar, 2008). In the cross-sectional study conducted in Maligita and Kibbi village of Uganda, husbands belonging to both villages believed that matters related to pregnancy and childbirth were the domain of women. And that husband's main responsibility was of provision of funds during pregnancy and childbirth (Singh, Lample & Earnest, 2014).

Further, studies by Sapkota, Kobayashi and Takase (2012) highlights mixed experiences of the husbands in the labor or delivery room (natal period), such as being positive towards attendants, hesitation, poor emotional reactions, being able to support, the need to be mentally prepared and enlightenment. Husbands reflected on their experiences positively, despite profound hesitation and overwhelming emotions. Tweheyo, Lule, Tumwesigye and Sekandi (2010) shows that 65.4% of husbands did participate in at least one antenatal check-up of their wives in Gulu district of Northern Uganda. They also shared that they got benefits from participation in antenatal check-ups with their wives such as awareness about HIV screening (74.5%), monitoring fetal growth (34%) and pregnancy related problems (18.9%). Kaye, Kakaire, Nakimuli, Osinde, Mabalinda and Kakande (2014) state that most husbands were willing to learn about their expected roles and support related to their wives during child birth in Mulago hospital, Uganda. A study by Mosunmola, Adekunbi and Foluso conducted in Ogun state, highlights that 96.5% of women agreed that husbands' support during pregnancy, labor and delivery was necessary and women felt encouraged by their husbands' support. (2014). The longitudinal study by Tinkew, Ryan, Carrano and Moore (2007) revealed that husbands who wanted the pregnancy sooner than it occurred are more likely to exhibit nurturing behavior toward their wives. On the other hand, 94.3% of husbands were present in the delivery room.

The above studies conclude that husband-participation may be influenced by the number of child births, unwanted/desired pregnancies, location of the couples, etc. Couples have started recognizing the benefits of husband-participation in maternal healthcare in term of acquiring knowledge, having positive attitudes, concerns, emotional support, roles and responsibilities and so on. In this scenario, it becomes necessary to question whether pregnancy and child care are only women's realm or the couple's domain.

Husband-Participation in Family Planning

Husband-participation in family planning is an essential factor for acceptance of temporary and permanent methods of contraceptives among partners. A study by Jayalakshmi, Ambwani, Prabhakar and Swain (2002), revealed that half of the husbands surveyed are the sole decision-makers regarding the number of children in their family in Delhi. Another study conducted in Delhi finds that educational status of the husband ensures active male involvement in family planning (Pathi, Rasania, Bhalla & Singh, 2004). A qualitative study by Mosha, Ruben and Kakoko (2013) finds that men decide on methods of family planning and the number of children in Mwanza of Tanzania. The data from Pakistan Demographic and Health Survey (1990-91) reveals that most men approve of use of family planning methods (Kiani & Framurz, 2003).

Further, a study conducted in Agra district of Uttar Pradesh by Khan and Patel (1997) brings out that 38% to 52% of the men surveyed mentioned that in their families all decisions related to family planning were taken by t h e husband alone. Another half felt that decisions were generally taken jointly with the wife and less than 10.0% felt that women alone make such decisions.

A study by Saini and Singh (2004) in Beri block, Rohtak of Haryana, brings out that most of the couples were using female-based family planning methods indicating poor male involvement in family planning. Another research shows that male involvement in family planning decision making was poor in Osun state of Nigeria (Ijadunolal, Abiona, Ijadunolal, Afolabi, Esimai & OlaOlorun, 2010).

The experimental research study conducted in Iran reveals that husbands' willingness to allow their wives to use family planning methods also increased, but use of family planning method was less in men even after intervention (Shahamfar, Kishor &Shokhvash, 2007). Another, study by Kaida, Kipp, Hessel and Kondelule (2005) Mpigi District, central Uganda, finds that husbands have limited knowledge about family planning and that almost all husbands approved of modern family planning and expressed great interest in participating. A study conducted with five generations of one South Indian, middle-class, high-caste family in Andhra Pradesh states that individual motivation rather than choice of methods of family planning is more important for positive male participation in family planning (Karra, Stark & Wolf,1997).

Thus, couple participation in family planning is required for proper interval between childbirths, which is helpful for a healthy mother and her new born child. Child bearing, rearing and spacing are responsibilities of both husband and wife. What is the situation of couple participation in adoption of family planning in Delhi?

Communication between Husband-Wife on Family Planning

Husband-wife or couple communication on family planning is most important for facilitating the efficient use of family planning methods or contraceptives among spouses. A study by Mukherjee (1975) shows that there is nonexistence of inter- spouse communication in matters pertaining to family planning in Meghalaya, Tamil Nadu and Haryana. It also brings out that absence of couple communication was more profound in rural areas than in urban areas. Another study by Koenig, Simmons and Misra (1984) shows that communication between spouses is lower among couples who use non-medical methods. Levels of communication are higher among couples who use medical methods such as condoms and contraception. Further, a study by Acharya and Sureender (1996) shows that husband-wife have good communication about family planning practices in Bihar (67.7%) and Tamil Naidu (70.2%). Kamal (1999) finds that use of modern contraceptives has increased because of frequent discussions between couples on family planning in Bangladesh. Only 29.2% of husband-wife never discuss the topic. Another study by Feyisetan (2000) brings out that usage of contraceptive is higher among marital partners where there is inter-spousal communication or who discuss and take joint decisions on contraception. Other studies revealed that better husband-wife communication has a significant role to play in the use of family planning methods. It also shows a strong positive impact of husband-wife communication on contraceptive use in Nepal (Azimi & Atiya, 2003 & Link, 2011).Further, a study by Berhane, Biadgilign, Amberbir, Morankar, Berhane and Deribe reveals that 60.3% of husbands had ever discussed family planning with their wives. Husband approval of family planning method is more likely to depend on couple communication on family planning in Angolela Tera District, Amhara Region of Ethiopia (2011). A cross sectional study conducted in Assosa Town of Ethiopia, finds that 82.0% of couples (one or both spouses) reported having communication on family planning (Zewditu, 2002). The data from Kenya Demographic and Health (1989) reveals that 83% of couples (one or both spouses) reported having family planning communication with their partners. It also leads to approval of use of family planning methods (Lasee & Becker, 1997). Another set of data from the Kenya Demographic and health survey (1998) finds that couple communication about family planning leads to improving knowledge of partner's attitude or in promoting approval (Dodoo, Ezeh & Owuor, 2001).

A review paper based on Pakistan Demographic and Health Survey (1990-1991) shows that a couple's approvals of family planning, knowledge of a source of family planning and communication about family planning are correlated with the desire to have limited number of children, and the association is particularly strong among couples in the rural areas (Mahmood & Ringheim1997). Another review study from the national level Pakistan Demographic and Health Survey (1990-91) states that the changes in husband's attitude, as well as exposure to family planning messages in the media, along with women's level of education are the main factors of generating couple communication about family planning. (Farooqui, 1994).

The data from Navrongo Health Research Centre (NHRC) panel surveys states that spousal communication does, indeed, promote use of contraceptive behavior, even when other factors are controlled (Bawah, 2002). The data from urban family life survey (1967) in Hong Kong, states that women with high level of couple communication are most likely to have desired pregnancies and thereby have fewer unwanted pregnancies (Mitchell, 1972). Further, study by Sharan and Thomas (2002) finds that in coupled who had not already been discussing family planning, exposure to relevant campaigns led to communication and use of family planning methods in Nepal. The study reveals that lack of communication between the husband and wife had an effecct on their acceptance of contraception, and whenever it occurred, it was initiated by the husband - that too after having two or three children, in Agra of Uttar Pradesh (Khan & Patel, 1997). A study by Kaida, Kipp, Hessel and Kondelule (2005) finds that spousal communication about familyplanning issues is generally poor in Mpigi District, central Uganda. A qualitative study by Mosha, Ruben and Kakoko (2013) finds that urban women shared family planning issues with their husbands as compared to rural areas where women could not speak about family planning issues before their partners in Mwanza of Tanzania.

The reviewed studies revealed that lack of couples communication leads to low usage of family planning methods while a high level of husband-wife communication has a positive impact in terms of better usage of family planning methods, as well as initiating joint decision-making on adoption of family planning. In general, couple communication plays a vital role in preventing unwanted pregnancies or multiple pregnancies.

Decision-making on Household and Maternal Healthcare Services

Decision-making is a crucial indicator to know about patterns related to household and maternal healthcare. The data from Nepal Demographic and health survey, 2001 revealed that husbands agreed that there is an association between the wife's autonomy and her use of healthcare services. Women's status in the household also determines usage of maternal healthcare services, other than joint decision-making associated with a higher level of husband-participation in pregnancy (Allendorf, 2007; Furuta & Salway, 2006 & Mullany, Hindin & Becker, 2005). Another study conducted in Kasulu district, Tanzania emphasized that couples should be involved in the decision-making process because it was related to increased deliveries at hospital (Danforth, Kruk, Rockers, Mbaruku & Galea, 2009). The study based survey report by Indonesia Family Life Survey (1997-98), states that those women who belong to high educational status and better social status are more likely to have a say in prenatal and delivery decision-making, as compared to women with low social and economic status in the family (Beegle, Frankenberg & Thomas, 2001). The study conducted in Kailali district of Nepal finds that increase in women's control over economic resources, in association with greater movement autonomy, would make maternal healthcare facilities more accessible to them (Thapa & Niehof, 2013). The study based on the Pakistan Social and Living Standards Measurement Survey (PSLM, 2005–06), finds that women's decision-making power has a significant positive correlation with use of maternal health services (Hou & Ma, 2013).

Further, a study states that women's decision-making related to freedom of movement leads to proper utilization of antenatal services and institutional delivery in urban areas ofVaranasi (Bloom, Wypij & Gupta, 2001). Another, study by Matthews, Brookes, Stones and Hossain (2005) finds that women who participated in the decision-making to purchase jewellery and other items were more than twice as likely as other women to have three or more antenatal check-up visits and institutional delivery in Mumbai. The study revealed that in women possessing major decision-making powers, health-seeking behavior was found to be higher (52.4%) in antenatal care, followed by immunization (39.61%). 38.7% women went for institutional delivery and 37.9% women were assisted by health professionals (Mahapatro, 2012). The Data from Ethiopia Demographic and Health Survey (EDHS, 2005) finds that women's decision-making has strong connections with the utilization of maternal healthcare services (Woldemicael & Tenkorang, 2010).

The study analysis based on National Family Health Survey–II (1998-99), states that rural Indian women have low level of decision-making which leads to low level of usage of maternal healthcare services (Mistry, Galal & Lu, 2009). The National Family Health Survey-III, 2005-06 states that less than one-third of women possess decision-making powers about their own healthcare (Kumar & Negi, No year). The data from Nepal Demographic and Health Survey, 2006 reveals that women from rural areas have less decision-making powers on major household purchases, own healthcare, purchase for daily household needs and visits to their family or relatives as compared to western women (Acharya, Bell, Simkhada, Teijlingen & Regmi, 2010). The household survey in 2003 by Guatemalan Maternal and Neonatal Health program, reveals that women have decision- making powers about household matters but that is not associated with health behavior practice during the maternal healthcare (Becker, Becker & Yglesias, 2006). The study conducted by Bangladesh Demographic and Health Survey (2007), finds that husband's participation was significantly lower in decision-making on household and maternal health issues (Story & Burgard, 2012).

The above studies find that education and economic status of women in family play a vital role in ensuring more decision-making powers related to household matters as well as maternal healthcare. Couple or joint decision-making is a positive trend to ensure proper use of maternal healthcare and husbands' involvement in pregnancy and post-partum care of their wives. In rural areas, women are still deprived of the power to make decisions or to have a say on household matters and maternal healthcare. After independence, women arestruggling to have a say in or gain power to make decisions on matters related to the household and maternal healthcare.

Relevance of the study

Husbands' participation in maternal healthcare of their wives has hardly gained any importance in Indian society. On the other hand, husband-participation in maternal health of their wives has been considered of critical importance in western countries.

Unfortunately, there is scant research on the husbands' involvement in family planning and reproductive healthcare of women. Although a few studies have considered the husbands' involvement in maternal healthcare of their wives, comprehensive research in this area covering husbands' participation in antenatal care, natal care and post natal care in terms of physical, economic, emotional, informational and couples communication during pregnancy has not been conducted.

Thus, considering the changing patterns of family and familial relations, the present research intends to understand couples' perspective on husband-participation in maternal healthcare. Husband-participation in maternal healthcare of their wife cannot be viewed in isolation. The family context becomes one of the significant indicators in all health- related aspects pertaining to women, especially maternal healthcare decisions, and their husband's participation in the same. Family belief and practice restrict or promote husband- participation in maternal healthcare of their wives. It is also essential to understand the family context that may have impact on husband-participation in maternal healthcare of their wives [for instance, role of mother-in-law or other family members in influencing decisions related to maternal and child healthcare]. The study has also tried to explore linkages between gender aspect and husband-participation. The present study has looked into various levels of husband-participation and also couples communication on maternal healthcare. It also examines various factors related to utilization or accessibility to maternal healthcare services by women in rural areas and slums of Delhi. The present research study also tried to look into the urban-rural locale difference in terms of couples' perspective on husband-participation in maternal healthcare of their wives. It is important to consider perspective of both husband and wife on husband-participation in maternal healthcare.

Research Methodology Significance of Present Research Work

It is of great significance to undertake the research on participation of husbands in maternal healthcare of their wives through the lens of social work research. Such a research can be helpful in reducing the maternal deaths or ensuring better health of mother and their new born child. This research would be helpful for social workers in understanding the connotation of husband-participation in maternal healthcare of their wives. Some studies have highlighted that maternal healthcare education and awareness among husbands would ensure greater involvement of men in the care of their wives during pregnancy. A study by Singh and Ram (2007) conducted in Uttar Pradesh reveals that women who share gynecological problems with their husbands were found to be more concerned and prompt in seeking treatment and those women who did not share their problems with their husbands are less likely to seek treatment. In this context, the present study looks into various aspects of husband-participation in maternal health care of their wives which leads to healthy women and their newborn children. This can also be helpful in reducing the maternal mortality rate and infant mortality rate. This research will be useful for various stakeholders in social work profession (such as medical social worker, community health worker, etc.) to understand or promote husband-participation in maternal healthcare towards proper usage of services and better health of pregnant women.

Objectives of the Study

General: - To study the couples' perspective on husband-participation in maternal healthcare services of the wives in rural areas and slums of Delhi.

Specific objectives

1. To understand the socio-demographic profile of the couple respondents in rural and slum areas of Delhi.
2. To assess the intra and extra familial factors related to accessibility to maternal healthcare services.
3. To study couple's perception towards the husband's involvement in maternal healthcare and their actual involvement in the maternal healthcare.
4. To appraise the level of communication between husband-wife regarding the issues pertaining to maternal healthcare and adoption of family planning measures.
5. To chalk out suggestive social work interventions for improving husbands' participation in maternal healthcare services.

In order to accomplish the objectives of the study, a triangulation of both qualitative and quantitative approaches has been used. This helps in generalizing relevant data that answer questions. The present study has adhered to descriptive research design as it focuses on describing the various aspects of couples' perspectives on husband-participation in maternal healthcare services.

Universe

The universe in the present study consists of all pregnant and lactating mothers (or mothers having infants) and their husbands in the National Capital Territory (NCT) of Delhi. For the present study, the researcher has used the probability method of cluster sampling technique for selecting the study area.

The present study focuses on Delhi, the National Capital Territory of India. Delhi is divided into nine districts and these districts have twenty seven sub-districts. Each and every district of Delhi has three sub-districts, like North West district has three sub-districts- Narela, Saraswati Vihar and Model Town. According to Census of Delhi (2011) report, of the total population residing in Delhi, 2.5% (4.19 million) is rural and 97.5% (1.67 billion) is urban. Further, seven districts of Delhi have both types of, rural and urban population and only two districts, i.e. New Delhi and Central Delhi districts have only urban population. According to census of Delhi 2011, 19 out of 27 sub-districts have urban population and only 8 out of 27 sub-districts have rural population residing in Delhi. According to Delhi Statistical Handbook (2012), there are one hundred twelve rural villages and one hundred of ten census towns in Delhi. There are 685 JJ (*jhuggi-jhopdi*) clusters in various districts of Delhi (Delhi Urban Shelter Improvement Board, 2011).

Scope of the Study

The reasons for choosing urban poor (slum) and rural population for the present study are as follows:-

a) The key indicators for urban poor in Delhi (National Family Health Survey-III, 2005-06) report show that there is a similarity in the level of awareness about maternal health services and literacy level among the urban poor (those living in designated slum areas, JJ cluster, unauthorized colonies, JJ resettlement colonies and regularized-unauthorized colonies) and that of the rural population in Delhi.

b) It is assumed that urban poor share similar socio-economic and cultural context with their rural counterparts as the latter group has recently migrated from rural areas.

c) Economically better off population groups have different socio-cultural and economic patterns of living, their utilization of maternal health services, family pattern, role distribution within family and intra familial resource allocation are very different than the urban poor and rural people (also see: Pathak et. al, 2001; Barua et. al, 2004; Pandey et. al, 2004 & Sagar, 2006;).

Selection of rural villages

For the purpose of the present study, a large population in the reproductive age group is required, as it would include only those parents who have up to one year old child. A large population is required for ensuring a representative sample needed for generalization in the present study. According to National Family Health Survey–III, 47.1% of rur al women in Delhi undergo institutional delivery (2005-06). It was important to understand rural couple's perspectives on husband-participation in maternal healthcare. Further, a large number of rural villages had to be visited to ascertain their suitability. As Narela and Najafgarh sub-districts of North West and south west districts of Delhi, have fulfilled most of the research requirements, these sites have been selected as the study areas. These two sub-districts come more or less closer to the requirement of homogeneity.

Selection of slum areas

The National Family Health Survey–III mentions that there were 16.6% institutional deliveries among women belonging to urban poor of Delhi (2005-06). The report of the Committee on Slum Statistic Census (2010), show that 18.9%t (2011 projected population) of slum population is residing in Delhi. Women living in slum communities face various problems due to lack of health facilities, unhygienic environment, lack of awareness about family planning, high numbers of home births, multiple pregnancies, etc., that directly and indirectly affect the women's maternal health. It was significant to understand the perspective of both husband and wife on husband-participation in maternal healthcare of the wife in the slum areas. In the present study, a large sample size has been a requirement, as it would include only those who fulfill inclusion criteria (parents who have up to one year old children) for the study. It also would require larger sample size for better representation that would be helpful for generalization of the present study. As South and North West of Delhi fulfills most of the research requirements, they have been selected as the study areas. These two districts come more or less closer to the requirement of homogeneity.

Profile of Holambi Kalan and Dichaon Kalan villages

North-West district is among the most populated districts of Delhi. In the north-west district, 89.66% males and 78.4% females are literate. For the present study, Holambi kalan village of Narela sub-district of north-west district of Delhi was taken as sample area. It is situated 2 km away from sub-district headquarter Alipur and 15 km away from district headquarter Kanjhawala. The total geographical area of village is 555.9 hectares (Census of India, 2011). According to District Census Handbook of Delhi (2014), its total population is 42,392 (22,933 males and 19,409 females) and has 8,457 households. Further, 15,014 males and 9,489 females are literate. There is one health dispensary within one km of the village. Holambi kalan village has adequate transport facilities.

Further, South-West district inhabits the third largest population of Delhi. Dichaon Kalan is one of the most populated villages of Najafgarh sub-district of South-west district of Delhi and it is situated 2 kms away from sub-district headquarter Najafgarh and 20 km away from district headquarter Kapashera. The total geographical area of the village is 1335.2 hectares. Total households in the village are 5,172 and its total population is 27,255, in which 14,255 are males and 12,702 females. Literacy rate among males is 11,715 and among females is 8,585 (Census of India, 2011). There is no dispensary or government run health service within the village premise. The transport facility in the village is grossly inadequate. In the present study, data gathered from both the villages were combined for rural areas.

Profile of Slum Areas

The population of slum dwellers is 17,85,390 in Delhi, of which 9,74,329 are males and 8,11,061 females. According to Directorate of Economic and Statistics (2014) in slums, there are 11,69,712 literate persons (males: 688085; females: 481627). For the present study, JJ camp Rakhi Market slum community of Zhakira was selected from North-West district of Delhi. This community has highest number of households, i.e. 5000, near railway land. There is government-run health dispensary within one km distance from Rakhi market community.

Another slum community, Navjeevan Camp & J.L. Nehru camp of Govind Puri, Kalkaji, was selected from South district of Delhi. The area has total 5000 households on Delhi Development Authority (DDA) land (Delhi Urban Shelter Improvement Board, 2011). Dispensary facilities by charitable organizations and government are available within one km of the slum community. Both slum communities are well connected with transport facilities. Both communities were combined for sample of slum areas for the present study.

Sampling Method

For the present study, samples of women and their husbands were drawn using non- probability method of quota sampling technique for the purpose of interview.

Inclusion Criterion: - Mother and father of infant up to one year.

Sample Size

The study has a sample size of 160 women. Sample frame was procured with the help of ASHA workers and *angandwadi* workers. The list was prepared and then prospective respondents were selected using quota sampling technique of non-probability method. Also, husbands of 160 women respondents were included in the study. Men or husband participating in the study were necessarily the spouse of women respondents in the study.

Table no. 1.04: Distribution of Sampled Areas and Sample Size

Respondents	*Narela sub-district (Rural)*	*Najafgarh sub-district (Rural)*	*South district (Slum)*	*North west District (slum)*	*Grand Total*
Women	40	40	40	40	160
And their	40	40	40	40	160
Total	80	80	80	80	320

For the present study, data was collected from both primary and secondary sources. The primary data collection was done with women and their husbands. Interview schedule was used for women and their husbands because it is a sensitive issue and there might be chances of women and their husbands being illiterate. Keeping these situations in mind, the researcher used the semi-structured interview schedule which contained both closed and open ended questions for more clarity. In the study, census data, National Family Health Survey-III and IV, Sample Registration System, etc. were included as secondary data. For the analysis of such secondary data comparisons, tables, charts and diagrams were done. For analyzing research studies including sources like books, journals, government documents, and so on systematic review was carried out. The researcher used the secondar y data from books, journals, government documents, and so on for the study. Secondary data has been gathered from various libraries in Delhi.

It had about 243 variables in women's schedule and 138 variables in husband's schedule. The coded data have been fed into SPSS 16.0 spread-sheet. Next, frequency and mean tables were developed and a number of cross-tables were taken out with a view to inter- relation between variables. The researcher applied various statistical tests such as central tendency, Dispersion, Correlation, Chi-square and t-test for slum and rural comparison among couples. In case of less than five values/cases/responses the researcher did not apply chi-square test ($\chi 2$). For the present study, the chi-square and t-test the researcher used only 95% of level of significance ($P<0.05$).

Chapter - 2

Utilization of Maternal Healthcare Services in Rural & Slum Areas

Motherhood is an important stage in the life of a woman and maternal health is a crucial aspect of this stage. Better maternal healthcare of a woman depends on many socio- demographic and economic factors. The factors like age at marriage, age at childbirth, religion, caste, type of family, education, income of husband, etc., influence health- seeking behavior of women during pregnancy and early child care. Studies by Dyson and Moore (1983), Jeffery and Basu (1996) support that women's health-seeking behavior is associated with several characteristics including their age, marital status, religion, and caste. In addition, women's status and autonomy are critical in promoting positive change in reproductive attitudes and behavior, especially in patriarchal societies. In the present study an attempt has been made to look into the socio- economic, demographic and cultural variables that influence maternal healthcare of women.

The present chapter looks into the comparative aspects of husband participation in the two locales—urban and rural. It analyses the differentials in variables related to husband participation in maternal healthcare—perception on husband social support, couple communication, decision-making on household matters and maternal healthcare etc. The chapter is divided into six parts. Part I covers socio-demographic profile of the couples, part II focuses on marital, maternal and child status, part III emphasizes utilization of maternal healthcare by rural and slum women, part IV reflects on factors affecting usage of maternal healthcare services by women in rural and slum areas and part V focuses on area -wise couple's views on husband- participation in maternal healthcare.

Part-I Socio-demographic profile of couples in slum and rural areas

This part reflects on age, education, occupation, monthly income, types of family, etc. of the husbands and their wives in rural and slum areas.

Age of couples

Table no. 2.01: Area-wise distribution of age of couples

Age (in years)	*No. of women*		*No. of men*	
	Slum (%)	Rural (%)	Slum (%)	Rural (%)
18-24	45 (56.3%)	25 (31.3%)	13 (16.2%)	9 (11.3%)
25-34	30 (37.5%)	55 (68.7%)	49 (61.3%)	62 (77.5%)
35 plus above	5 (6.2%)	-	18 (22.5%)	9 (11.2%)
Total	80 (100%)	80 (100%)	80 (100%)	80 (100%)

Table 2.01 shows that in slums, women in the youngest age category are more while in the age category of 25 to 34 years women from rural areas show higher proportion. Further, the distribution of men in the two areas in different age groups shows similarity.

Educational status of women and husbands

Table no. 2.02 :Area-wise distribution of educational status of women and men

Educational status of women	*No. of women*		*No. of men*	
	Slum (%)	*Rural (%)*	*Slum (%)*	*Rural (%)*
Illiterate	31 (38.8%)	4 (5%)	22 (27.5%)	-
School	46 (57.5%)	60 (75%)	55 (68.7%)	64 (80%)
College	3 (3.7%)	16 (20%)	3 (3.8%)	16 (20%)

Table 2.02 presents details of area-wise distribution of educational status of men and women. It shows that men and women in urban slums have higher proportions of illiteracy than rural inhabitants. Women's educational levels are significantly lower than their male counterparts. This trend becomes sharper with increasing educational levels. Thus, women from slum areas are educationally most backward.

Area-wise distribution of occupation of women

In the present study, most (97.5%) women from slum areas were housewives and only 2.5% of them were working (*Anganwadi* worker & home-based work). The highest proportions (95%) of women respondents from rural areas were housewives. Only 5 percent of respondents belonging to rural areas were working (teachers & ANMs).

Area-wise distribution of religion and caste of couples

The majority (78.8%) of the couples from urban slums were Hindus and 21.2% professed Islam. Also, most (96.2%) rural couples were Hindus and only 3.8% Muslim.

Caste distribution shows that 20% of respondents in urban and 12.5% in rural areas were from general category. Next, 40% of slum couples and 33.8% of rural couples were Scheduled Castes. Another, more than a-half (52.5%) of couples in rural and 5% in slum areas belonged to Other Backward Classes (OBCs). Only 2.5% of slum couples are Scheduled Tribes and none of them were in rural areas. Likewise, 8.8% of couples in slum and 1.2% of them in rural areas were from other caste category. Rest (23.7%) of the slum couples did not respond to the question about caste.

Native state of couples

In the slum areas, 48.8% of couples were from Uttar Pradesh, 20% from Bihar, 15% from Rajasthan, 5% from West Bengal, 2.5% from Uttaranchal and 1.2% each from Haryana, Madras, Orissa, Kolkata, Ranchi and Delhi. Only 1.3 percent of couple did not respond on the same. In the rural areas, 1.2% of couples were from Uttar Pradesh, 1.2% from Bihar, 3.8% from West Bengal, 2.5% from Haryana and 91.3% from Delhi. In the study, most of the slum couples belonged to Uttar Pradesh and most of the rural couples belonged to Delhi.

Types of family of couples

In the study, little less than a half (46.2%) of slum couples belong to joint families. On the other hand, majority (77.5%) of couples from rural areas stay in joint families. Next, 53.8% of couples in slums live in nuclear families. Only 22.5% of rural couples are staying in nuclear families.

Data brings out that more rural couples belong to joint family system as compared to slum couples. Migration and search for better livelihood can be reasons for formation ofnuclear family in slum areas. Joint family system still exists in rural areas. In the study, 47.5% of couples from slum areas had 3 to 5 members and 52.5% had more than 5 members in their families. In the rural areas, 33.8% of couples had 3 to 5 members and 66.2% had more than 5 members in their household.

Area-wise types of house of couples

In the slum areas, more than a half (58.8%) of couples were staying in *pucca* houses, 16.2% of them in half-thatched houses and 25% in rented houses. Most (97.5%) of the couples were from rural areas living in *pucca* houses and only 2.5% of them were in half-thatched houses. In rural areas all the couples have their own houses.

Occupational status of husbands

Table no. 2. 03: Area-wise distribution of occupational status of husbands

Occupation	*No. of husbands*			
	Slum	*Percent (%)*	*Rural*	*Percent (%)*
Government	-	-	10	12.5
Private	52	65	37	46.3
Business	15	18.8	18	22.5
Daily wager	12	15	5	6.2
Farmer	-	-	7	8.8
No work due illness	1	1.2	-	-
Studying	-	-	1	1.2
Unemployed	-	-	2	2.5
Total	80	100	80	100

Table no. (2.03) provides details of area -wise occupational status of husbands. It reflects that men from urban slums have a higher proportion of private jobs while a size-able proportion of rural men are in government jobs.

Monthly income of husbands

In the study, majority (78.8%) of husbands in slum areas had monthly income below Rs. 10000 and more than half (61.3%) of rural husbands had monthly income more than 10000 rupees. In rural areas, husbands have better socio-economic status as compared to husbands from slums.

Part- II Marital, maternal and child status

This part focuses on age at marriage, age at first childbirth, birth weight of child and so on.

Women's age at marriage

Table no. 2.04: Distribution of women's age at marriage

Age (in years)	*No. of women*			
	Slum	*Percent (%)*	*Rural*	*Percent (%)*
Below 18	26	32.5	5	6.3
18-29	52	65	75	93.7
NA/NR/DK	2	2.5	-	-
Total	80	100	80	100

In the study, 32.5% of women in slum areas and only 6.3% of rural women were married before 18 years. More than half (65%) of wo men in slum areas and most (93.7%) of women in rural areas were marr ied in age gr oup of 18 to 29 year s. Similar trends are observed by Chandha (1989) who finds that two-thirds of the women had married before 18 years of age in resettlement colonies of Delhi. The mean age at marriage of slum women is 18.37 years and in rural women age at marriage is 20.75 years.

Husbands' age at marriage

In the present study, 27.5% of men from urban slums and 13.7% from rural areas were married before 21 years of age. More than a half (67.5%) of men from slums and most (82.5%) of the men from rural areas were married in age group of 21 to 29 years. Equal proportion (3.8%) of men in slums and rural areas were married in age group of 30 to 36 years. Rest (1.2%) of man from slum was did not respond. Rural men more frequently get married after the legal age of marriage in contrast to urban slums. The mean age at marriage of men from slum areas is 22.62 years and for men from rural areas mean age is 24.27 years.

First pregnancy

In slum areas, 12.5% women conceived their first child within one to three months, 20% in four to six months, 13.8% within one year of marriage, 8.8% within one year of marriage but had miscarriage, 41.2% after one year of marriage and 3.7% did not remember. In rural areas, 30% of women conceived their first child within one to three months, 16.2% in four to six months, 5% within one year of marriage, 10% within one year of marriage but had miscarriage and 38.8% of them conceived their first child after one year of marriage. There is no significant difference between women's first pregnancy based on area (slum and rural).

Adoption of family planning method before first childbirth

In the study, most of the (95%) women from slum areas did not adopt any family planning methods before the first childbirth. Only 2.5% planned their first child and condom was the most preferred family planning method. Further, 2.5 percent of women from slums did not respond for the same. On the other hand, 100% women in rural areas did not adopt any family planning methods before the first child birth. Delay of first pregnancy of women is never promoted in Indian culture.

Women's age at first child birth

Table no. 2.05: Area-wise distribution of women's age at first childbirth

Age (in years)	*No. of women*			
	Slum	*Percent (%)*	*Rural*	*Percent (%)*
14–19	31	38.8	10	12.5
20-24	42	52.5	53	66.2
25-29	5	6.2	15	18.8
30 plus	-	-	2	2.5
NA/NR/DK	2	2.5	-	-
Total	80	100	80	100

The table no. (2.05) presents area -wise information on women's age at first child birth. Results show that women from urban slums more frequently had their first child at or before 19 years of age in contrast to rural women. Early marriage and early childbearing practice is more commonly seen among women from slum areas. A study conducted in Gujarat State finds that 22% of women in urban slums and 11% of them in rural areas had their first childbirth before the age of 18 years (Gandotra & Dey, 2011). The mean age of slum women at their first child birth is20.75 years and among rural women it is 22.45 years.

Planned first child

In the study, most (93.8%) of the women in slum and rural (96.2%) areas had planned their first child. Only 6.2% slum women and 3.8% rural women did not plan their first child.

Area-wise stillbirth or infant death

In the present study, only 6.2% of slum in women reported that they had stillbirths while no case of stillbirth was reported in rural areas and 5% of women from slums and 2.5% from rural areas had experienced infant death. Equal proportion (1.2%) of women in slum and rural areas had experienced both stillbirth and infant death.

Women's maternal status

The data shows that 16.2% of slum women had pre-term childbirth in contrast to 31.2% rural women. Study results show that 18.8% women from slums and 27.5% from rural areas had childbirth through operation. Late pregnancy can be reason for the childbirth through operation.

Birth weight

Study results bring out that 25% of women from slum areas had under-weight (less than 2.5 kg) children at birth in comparison to 12.5% rural women with under-weight neonates. Rest of the women were in NA/DK/NR category. According to National Family Health Survey –III (2005-06) 21.5% women have less than2.5 Kg weight of child at birth in Delhi.

Childbirth spacing

In the study, 22.5% of women from slum areas and 12.5% of rural women had less than two years interval between last two children. Further, 47.5% of slum women and 43.8% of rural women had childbirth spacing of more than two years. Rest were in NA/DK/NR category.

Number of children

In the present study, 67.5% of women in slums and 83.8% in rural areas have two children or one. Likewise, 32.5% slum women and 16.2% rural women have more than two children. Study trends show that rural women are more likely to have small families as compared to women from slums.

Part-III Usage of Maternal Healthcare Services

This part deals with usage of ANC visits, institutional delivery, child immunization, adoption of family planning methods, etc., by women from rural and slum areas.

Maternal healthcare services by women

Table 2.06 gives area-wise details of usage of maternal healthcare services by women in the current (last) pregnancy. It shows that except ANC visits and Tetanus injections, women from slum areas lag behind rural women in usage of maternal health services. Delhi State Report (2009) shows that 66.6% of slum women have childbirth at home in contrast to 53% rural women. Further, a study by Archana, Nikhil, Singh, Palanivel and Nongkynrih (2010) brings out that there were 85.4% institutional deliveries and 14.6% home deliveries in a resettlement colony of south Delhi. The researcher analyzed that most of the women in slum areas were dependent on government health centers for utilization of maternal healthcare, may be due to economic constraints. In the present study rural women utilized both government and private health services during their pregnancy, deliver y and child immunization.

Table no. 2.06 : Area-wise distribution of use of maternal healthcare services

Maternal health services	*No. of women*			
	Slum		*Rural*	
	Yes (%)	*No (%)*	*Yes (%)*	*No (%)*
Antenatal check-up	80 (100%)	-	80 (100%)	-
T T Injection	80 (100%)	-	80 (100%)	-
Acid tablets	74 (92.5%)	6 (7.5%)	80 (100%)	-
Institutional delivery	56 (70%)	24 (30%)	78 (97.5%)	2 (2.5%)
Child immunization	73 (91.2%)	7 (8.8%)	80 (100%)	-
Family planning information	25 (31.2%)	55 (68.8%)	35 (43.8%)	45 (56.2%)
Visits of health visitor	7 (8.8%)	73 (91.2%)	37 (46.2%)	42 (52.6%)

Women's health-related problems

Study results show that in the slum areas, 17.5% of women had pregnancy-related health problems in comparison to 16.2 % rural women. Next, 11.2% women from slums and only 1.2% from rural areas had delivery-related problems. Further, 11.2% women from slums and 7.5% from rural dwellings had health problems post-delivery. Data also show that 18.8% of children from slums and 7.5% of rural newborn children had health-related problems. It shows that slum women and their newborn children tend to have a larger share of health-related problems during pregnancy, delivery and after childbirth. Reason for this may be poor intake of nutritious food, no proper rest, inadequate family support in household work, unhygienic environment, etc.

Area-wise adoption of family planning methods by women

In the present study, 21.2 % slum women were using family planning methods such as condoms (12.5%), female operations (3.8%), copper-T (3.8%), pills (1.2%) and 78.8% of them did not adopt any methods of family planning. In rural areas, 28.8% of women were using methods of family planning like condoms (7.5%), female operation (3.8%), Copper-T (15%), pills (2.5%) and 70% of them did not adopt any. Thus, rural women have shown slightly higher usage of family planning methods over women from urban slums.

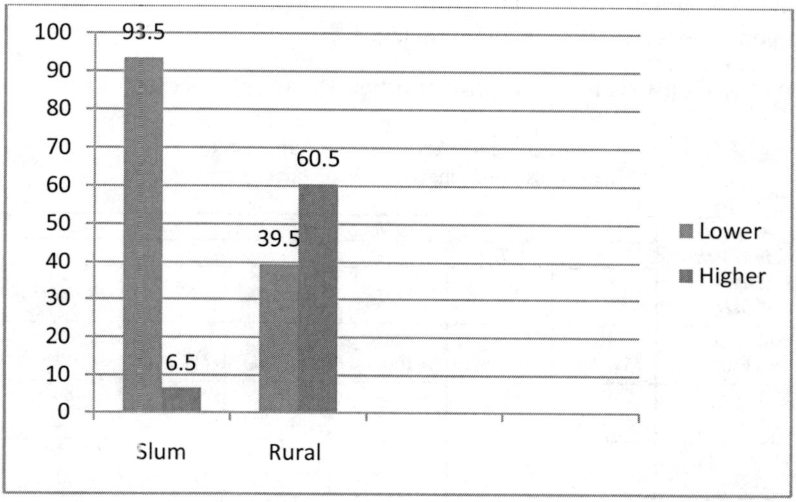

Figure no. 2.01 Locale-wise level of use of maternal healthcare services.

Use of maternal healthcare services

The above figure (no. 2.01) presents area -wise details of level of use of maternal healthcare services. It vividly shows that rural women have much better usage of health services than women from slum areas. Relevant statistics confirm the same (Contingency Coefficient = 0.393 and Spearman Correlation = 0.427). There is a statistically significant difference between rural-urban locale and utilization of maternal healthcare services (χ^2=29.167, P<0.05).

Part-IV Factors affecting maternal healthcare of women

This part covers the awareness about maternal healthcare programs, services, food restrictions during pregnancy and after delivery, availability of health services, etc. in the context of rural and slum areas.

Awareness and benefits related to maternal healthcare

Most women (91.2% from slum and 92.5% from rural areas) were not aware of any maternal health–related programmes and schemes. Only a few were aware of these [IGMSY: 1.2% from slums; Janani Suraksha Yojana: 2.5% from rural; Do not know both these programmes: 7.6% from slums, 5% rural]. Another, 98.8% of slum and rural women did not get any benefits of maternal health programmes. Only 1.2 percent of women from slums and 1.2 percent of them from rural areas get benefit of maternal health. In the study, there is no significant difference between awareness and getting benefits of maternal healthcare programmes by Government among women from slum and rural areas.

Women's awareness on maternal healthcare services

Table no. 2.07 Area-wise distribution of awareness about maternal healthcare services

Awareness about three stages of MHC	*No. of women*					
	Slum			*Rural*		
	Yes (%)	*No (%)*	*Total (%)*	*Yes (%)*	*No (%)*	*Total (%)*
Antenatal check-up	46 (57.5%)	34 (42.5%)	80 (100%)	71 (88.8%)	9 (11.2%)	80 (100%)
Delivery	47 (58.8%)	33 (41.2%)	80 (100%)	71 (88.8%)	9 (11.2%)	80 (100%)
Post-natal check-up	45 (56.2%)	35 (43.8%)	80 (100%)	70 (87.5%)	10 (12.5%)	80 (100%)

Table no (2.07) gives area -wise details of women's awareness about maternal healthcare services. It clearly shows that women from slums lag behind their rural counterparts in terms of awareness about maternal healthcare services (antenatal care = Spearman Correlation=0.352; natal care: Spearman Correlation =0.341 and post natal care: Spearman Correlation =0.348). There is a significant difference between locale of women and awareness about maternal healthcare services (antenatal care: $\chi 2=19.877$, $P<0.05$; natal care: $\chi 2=18.596$, $P<0.05$ and post-natal care: $\chi 2=19.324$, $P<0.05$). Further, women from slums are a more contributing factor in terms of lack of awareness about natal and post-natal care services (Standard Residual= +2.6) while fewer rural women are contributing to lack of awareness related to natal and post-natal care services (Standard Residual = -2.6). Further, related to antenatal care, slum women are a greater contributing factor in lack of awareness (Standard Residual = +2.7). Likewise, rural women are less contributing factor to lack of awareness related to antenatal care services (Standard Residual = -2.7).

Food and restrictions

Results of the study show that almost all (98.8% during pregnancy and 100% after child birth) the rural women and most of the slum women (85% during pregnancy and 87.5% after child birth) had extra food intake during pregnancy. Equal proportion (3.8%) of rural and urban women had diet restrictions during pregnancy phase due to health problems or cultural norms.

And 26.2% rural, 2.5% women from slums had food restrictions after child-birth. Poverty and economic constraints are probably the reason for lower intake of extra food by the pregnant and lactating mothers in urban slums.

Child delivery at home

In the present study, 8.8% of women from slums were forced to give birth at home. In rural areas, only 2.5% (two) of them were forced to give birth at home.

Women's faith in traditional birth-attendants

Results show that 33.8% women from slums and 5% rural women have faith in traditional *dais*. The reasons cited are easy affordability, and comfort (27.5percent), saving of time(1.2%), hospitals insist on operation (1.2%), saving of money (1.2%), and that managing one's household is easier in home-delivery (1.2%). Another study by Sagar (2006) brings out that many (60%) women in slums preferred home delivery by *dais* because they remain within the comfort of familiar surroundings, with easy availability of elder women of their house and neighborhood to give support or advice if needed.

Heavy household work during pregnancy and family support

In the slum areas, 28.8% of women and only 10% rural women were engaged in heavy household work during the pregnancy. Further, majority (70%) of slum women were getting help from other family members such as mothers-in-law (46.2%) and husbands (23.8%), and 30% of them did not get help from other family members for managing household work. Only 6.2% of rural women did not get help and 93.8% of them got help from other family members including mothers-in-law (70%) and husbands (23.8%) for managing household work. Joint family support system is frequently available in rural areas.

Fetching water

In the present study, most (83.8%) of the slum women and 95% of rural women did not go for taking or fetching. Only 16.2% of women in slums went outside home for taking/fetching water from a source within 1 km range (15.2%) for up to five months (1.2%), six to eight months (2.5%) and nine to ten months (12.5%) during their pregnancy. Another, 5% of women in rural area went outside the home for taking /fetching water from a source near their home for up to nine to ten months of their pregnancy. There are inadequate basic civic amenities in slum areas as compared to rural areas.

Rest time

In slum areas, most (93.8%) women in slum areas and 97.5% in rural areas were getting proper time for rest during pregnancy. Only 6.2% of slum women did not get proper time due to household work constraints (1.2%) and rest of them did not respond (5%). Next, 2.5% of rural women did not get proper rest time due to household work constraints (1.2%) and rest of them did not respond (1.2%).

Health facility: Distance

Results show that all (100%) the women from slum areas mentioned about availability of healthcare including dispensary (97.5%) and private clinic (2.5%) within one km. Next,majority (76.2%) of rural women reported availability of health system such as dispensary (76.2%) within one km, 15% of them did not have availability of it and rest were in do not know category (8.8%).

Milestones of child development

Table no. 2.08: Area-wise distribution of milestone of child development

Milestone of child development	*No. of children*			
	Slum		*Rural*	
	On time	*Delay*	*On time*	*Delay*
Motor Development	37 (55.2%)	30 (44.8%)	40 (64.5%)	22 (35.5%)
Language Development	33 (55%)	27 (45%)	32 (59.3%)	22 (40.7%)
Adaptive Development	31 (52.5%)	28 (47.5%)	31 (58.5%)	22 (41.5%)
Socio-Personal Development	44 (62%)	27 (38%)	46 (66.7%)	23 (33.3%)

Table no. 2.08 gives details of area-wise milestone of child development. Study reveals that there is marginal difference in motor, language, adaptive and socio-personal development of slum and rural children.

In the present chapter, socio-economic and demographic factors influencing maternal health have been delineated. It helped in understanding the respondents' background. These socio- economic characteristics of couples give the context in which we would be looking into factors influencing the proper utilization of maternal healthcare services. There are various intra- and extra- familial factors affecting the usage of pregnancy care service which directly and indirectly influence the health of pregnant women.

Chapter - 3

Husband- A Critical Actor in Maternal Healthcare Services

Husband's support and participation are crucial for the betterment of his wife's psychological, physical and social aspects of life. This is all the more applicable for reproductive and maternal health, especially during and after the delivery of the child. However, in traditional societies where a patriarchal system dominates, overt participation of a husband in caring for his wife has been frowned upon. Nonetheless, across the world, social scientists, health experts and policy makers are increasingly confirming positive impacts of husband's pro-active role in wife's care during pregnancy and after childbirth. According to the Beijing Declaration and the Platform for Action (Fourth Conference), emphasis is laid on encouraging men to share equal responsibilities in child-care and household work and to provide their share of financial support for their families, even if they do not live with them (1996). It is important that men must share the maternal health and child care responsibility and should break the social barriers that prevent husband's participation in activities that culturally are considered 'women's domain'.

In the present study, an attempt has been made to look into the rural and slum couples' views on husband-participation in physical, economic, informational support, overall husband- participation in maternal healthcare and perception of husband support in maternal healthcare.

Scale- Couples' perception of husband support on maternal healthcare

Here, women and men respondents' perceptions of husband support on maternal healthcare are studied. For developing a scale, 84 statements were formulated covering perceptions or perspectives of the couple on the support to be provided to the wife during pregnancy and childbirth on various parameters. After pretesting, 22 statements which have maximum discriminable power have been retained on the scale. There are five positive and seventeen negative statements in the scale.

Couples' perception of husband support on maternal healthcare

Table no. 3.01 : Area-wise distribution of couples' perception of husband support in maternal healthcare.

Statements	*No. of couples*					
	Slum			*Rural*		
	Agreed (%)	*Disagree (%)*	*Uncertain (%)*	*Agreed (%)*	*Disagree (%)*	*Uncertain (%)*
Physical Support						
It is not the responsibility of husband to accompany his wife during prenatal or ANC visits.	28 (17.5%)	102 (63.8%)	30 (18.7%)	6 (3.7%)	148 (92.5%)	6 (3.8%)
Women should be able to go alone for all ANC visits during pregnancy.	88 (55%)	61 (38.1%)	11 (6.9%)	37 (23.1%)	118 (73.8%)	5 (3.1%)
Husband should accompany his wife for any prenatal or antenatal check-up visits during pregnancy.	132 (82.5%)	15 (9.4%)	13 (8.1%)	157 (98.1%)	2 (1.3%)	1 (0.6%)
Man/husband should help in heavy household work during pregnancy.	132 (82.5%)	20 (12.5%)	8 (5%)	149 (93.1%)	7 (4.4%)	4 (2.5%)
Man /husband is needed to help his wife in managing the older children after delivery.	146 (91.2%)	8 (5%)	6 (3.8%)	149 (93.1%)	10 (6.3%)	1 (0.6%)
It is not fathers' responsibility to change nappies, feed, give bath, etc., to their newborn child.	28 (17.5%)	125 (78.1%)	7 (4.4%)	36 (22.5%)	121 (75.6%)	3 (1.9%)
Woman should not ask her husband to accompany her for immunization of newborn child.	51 (31.9%)	88 (55%)	21 (13.1%)	15 (9.3%)	139 (86.9%)	6 (3.8%)
Economic support						
It is justified for a man to get angry if his wife asks for money for pregnancy related expenses.	35 (21.9%)	93 (58.1%)	32 (20%)	13 (8.1%)	135 (84.4%)	12 (7.5%)
Family members (in-laws) are not responsible in fulfilling financial needs of pregnant woman.	43 (26.9%)	100 (62.5%)	17 (10.6%)	85 (53.1%)	68 (42.5%)	7 (4.4%)
There is no need of medical expenses during pregnancy or delivery because government provides free of cost facilities.	73 (45.6%)	62 (38.8%)	25 (15.6%)	81 (50.6%)	62 (38.8%)	17 (10.6%)
Informational support/Communication/Emotional Support						
Husband is not required to ask his wife about common health problems during pregnancy.	17 (10.6%)	127 (79.4%)	16 (10%)	6 (3.8%)	149 (93.1%)	5 (3.1%)

Woman should take care of herself during pregnancy, husband's inference/advice is not needed.	48 (30%)	90 (56.2%)	22 (13.8%)	45 (28.1%)	102 (63.8%)	13 (8.1%)
Husband/man should give advice about importance of intake of medicine during gus wife's	146 (91.2%)	4 (2.5%)	10 (6.3%)	154 (96.3%)	5 (3.1%)	1 (0.6%)
It is not husband's domain to give advice on pregnancy care to his wife.	22 (13.8%)	107 (66.9%)	31 (19.3%)	24 (15%)	127 (79.4%)	9 (5.6%)
Wife should not share common problems during pregnancy with her husband and disturb him.	84 (52.5%)	61 (38.1%)	15 (9.4%)	32 (20%)	116 (72.5%)	12 (12.5%)
There is no need to discuss with husband about the process related to childbirth. These are the woman's own feelings.	30 (18.8%)	102 (63.8%)	28 (17.4%)	20 (12.5%)	123 (76.9%)	17 (10.6%)
Discussion on Family planning						
It is fine for a woman to initiate discussion on family planning with her husband.	125 (78.1%)	14 (8.8%)	21 (13.1%)	153 (95.6%)	6 (3.8%)	1 (0.6%)
If a woman tells her husband to use a condom, he often gets angry.	36 (22.5%)	70 (43.8%)	54 (33.7%)	17 (10.6%)	110 (68.8%)	33 (20.6%)
If woman initiates talk on use of family planning methods with her husband, it ultimately leads to fighting.	38 (23.8%)	86 (53.8%)	36 (22.4%)	16 (10%)	129 (80.6%)	15 (9.4%)
A woman from good family never talks freely about family planning with her husband.	26 (16.2%)	55 (34.4%)	79 (49.4%)	20 (12.5%)	100 (62.5%)	40 (25%)
Woman should not discuss with husband about family planning.	29 (18.1%)	74 (46.3%)	57 (35.6%)	22 (13.8%)	97 (60.6%)	41 (25.6%)
Women are born only for bearing and rearing children.	45 (28.1%)	103 (64.4%)	12 (7.5%)	20 (12.5%)	123 (76.9%)	17 (10.6%)

Table (no. 3.01) gives details of slum and rural couples' perception of husband support in maternal healthcare. The scale has four dimensions– physical (accompanying for ANC), economic support, informational/ emotional/communication and discussion on family planning. In the study, rural couples have positive outlook related to perception of husband support in maternal healthcare as compared to their counterpart slum couples.

Physical Support: On a statement 'It is not the responsibility of husband to accompany his wife during prenatal or ANC visits', more than half (63.8%) of couples in slums and most (92.5%) of rural couples disagreed. Whereas on a statement 'women should be able to go alone for all ANC visits during pregnancy', more than half (55%) of couples in slums and only 23.1% of rural couples agreed. Next, on a statement 'husband should accompany his wife for any prenatal or antenatal check-up visits during pregnancy, 82.5% of couples in slums and most (98.1%) rural couples agreed. Further, on a statement 'man/husband should help in heavy household work during pregnancy', 12.5% of couples in slums and 4.4% of rural couples disagreed. Another, on a statement 'man /husband is needed to help his wife in managing the older children after delivery', 5% of couples in slums and 6.3% of rural couples disagreed. On the other hand, on a statement 'it is not fathers' responsibility to change nappies, feed, bathe, their newborn child', 17.5% of couples in slums and 22.5% of rural couples agreed. Likewise, on a statement 'woman should not ask her husband to accompany her for immunization of newborn child', 31.9% of couples from slums and 9.3% of rural couples agreed.

Economic Support: On a statement on the theme of economic support, 'it is justified for a man to get angry if his wife asks money for pregnancy-related expenses' more than half (58.1%) of couples from urban slums and most (84.4%) of rural couples disagreed. On the other hand, on a statement 'family members (in-laws) are not responsible in fulfilling financial needs of pregnant woman', 62.5% of couples from slums and 42.5% of rural couples disagreed. Further, on a statement 'there is no need of medical expenses during pregnancy or delivery because government provides free of cost facilities', 45.6% of couples from slums and 50.6% of rural couples agreed.

Informational support/Communication/Emotional Support: Further, on informational support/ communication theme, 79.4% of couples from slums and 93.1% rural couples agreed on a statement that 'husband is not required to ask his wife about common health problems during pregnancy'. Only 30% of couples from slums and 28.1% rural couples agreed on a statement that 'woman should take care of herself during pregnancy, husband's inference /advice is not needed'. On the other hand, 91.2% of couples from slums and 96.3% of rural couples agreed on a statement that 'husband/man should give advice about importance of intake of medicine during his wife's pregnancy'. About two-thirds (66.9%) of couples from slums and 79.4% of rural couples disagreed on a statement that 'it is not husband's domain to give advice on pregnancy care to his wife'. Further, 52.5% of couples from slums and 20% of rural couples agreed on a statement that 'wife should not share about common problems during pregnancy with her husband and disturb him. Whereas 63.8% of couples from slums and 76.9% of rural couples disagreed on the statement that 'there is no need to discuss with your husband about the process related to childbirth. These are a woman's own feelings'.

Family Planning: The theme related to discussion on family planning, on a statement 'it is fine for a woman to initiate discussion on family planning with her husband' majority (78.1%) of couples from slums and 95.6% of rural couples agreed. Next, 22.5% of couples in urban slums and 10.6% of rural couples agreed on a statement that 'if a woman tells her husband to use condom, he often gets angry'. Whereas 23.8% of couples from slums and.

Natal care/Delivery: Husband's presence during delivery is significant for providing emotional support to the wife. Majority (79.4%) of males from slums were present at time of childbirth and 20.6% of them were not present. Whereas most (96.9%) of rural males were present at time of delivery and only 3.1% of them did not accompany their wife for the same.

Child immunization: Husband accompanying the wife for child immunization often reflects his concerns for the health of his newborn baby. In the study 31.3% of males from slums accompanied and 68.1% of them did not accompany their wives for child immunization. Only 0.6% of male from slum did not respond. On the other hand, most (82.5%) males from rural accompanied their wives for child immunization and only 17.5% of them did not accompany them for the same.

Household work: It may help a woman to get proper time for rest, thereby ensuring better health of mother and newborn child. More than half (61.2%) of men from slums were engaged in household work. Only 38.8% of males from slum areas did not participate in household work. Likewise, 65.6% of rural males helped in household work and 34.4% of them did not participate.

Husbands' help in caring for older children: A pregnant woman often requires help in the care of older children such as getting them ready for school, dropping them to school, feeding, bathing and so on. Traditionally, in India, child-care has been viewed as women's job. It was against the prevalent traditional norms of manhood to tend young children, feed them and bathe them. More than half (56.2%) of males in slums helped in caring for older children and 28.8% of them did not help with the same. Only 15% of males in slums did not respond. On the other hand, 43.7% of rural males helped and 33.8% of them did not help in caring for older children. Next, 22.5% of rural males did not respond.

Case study 3.01

Husband willing to support but job constraints

Rahim (name changed) is a thirty-two-year-old 32 years old man working in a private company on a monthly salary of 14000 rupees only. He stays in a joint family in rural Delhi and has three sons.

Rahim is frustrated that because of his demanding job, he is unable to provide support to his wife. He desperately wanted to accompany his wife to the doctor for health check-ups but his long and erratic working hours do not permit him to do so.

Moreover, he mentioned that initially, he took leave from office and accompanied his wife to the doctor, but she did not let him enter her cabin and allowed only his wife in. He has complaints against the doctors and healthcare staff of government hospitals who do not allow husbands to be with their pregnant wives, and yet keep on shouting that men too should be responsible and supportive.

Economic support

Money for Travel Expenses: In the study, 39.4% of women from slums received money from their husband and only 8.8% of them were helped by family relatives to meet travel expenses for ANC visits. More than half (51.8%) of the women in slums did not require travel expenses due to close proximity of the health center or dispensary. On the other hand, majority (77.5%) of rural women received money from their husband and 10% of them are helped by family relatives to meet travel expenses for ANC visits. While 12.5% of rural women did not require travel expenses due to close proximity of the health center or dispensary. Thus, in the study, none of the respondents were left unaided for want of travel expenses.

Medicines and Other Medical Check-Up: Majority (74.4%) of women from slums got money for buying medicines and other medical check-up requirements from their husbands. Only one (0.6%) woman from slum did not get money for the same because of inadequate income of her husband. Only 5.6% of women in slum areas have received the economic support for medical requirements from their family relatives. Next, 19.4% of women in slums cited that they did not require money for medical checkups requirements because of free of cost medicines available in health set-ups. Whereas 75% of rural women got money for buying medicines and other medical check-up requirements from their husbands and 5% of them received money for the same from their family members. Further, 20% of women mentioned that they did not require money for medical checkups requirements because of free of cost medicines available in health set-ups.

Extra Nutritional Food: Most (81.9%) of the women in slums received money for extra nutritional food intake from their husbands and 13.1% of them got money from their family relatives for the same. Only 5.0% of women did not get money for this purpose from their husbands due to insufficient money/income. On the other hand, 70.6% of rural women received money for extra nutritional food intake from their husbands. Another 29.4% of rural women got money for extra nutritional food intake by their family relatives.

Case study 3.02

Insufficient Income

Rajesh (name changed), 28 years, migrant from Bihar is a taxi driver. He lives in a *jhuggi* in a Delhi slum with his wife and two children. He is able to earn 8000 rupees and has several expenditures that make him perpetually long for more money. His job constraints did not allow him to help his wife during her pregnancy and there was nobody else to support his wife. He feels the pinch that he was not able to earn enough to provide nutritional food to his wife during pregnancy.

Informational Support

In the present study, there being various sources of information such as formal system (including doctors, ANMs, ASHA workers and *anganwadi* workers) and informal system (mother-in-laws, family relatives), women already had information. There are some instances where husbands did not have information on maternal healthcare services.

Antenatal check-up visits: In the study, 38.8% of couples in slums got and 61.2% of them did not receive information related to antenatal check-up visits. More than half (58.1%) of rural couples were provided with information during their antenatal check-up visits and 41.9% of them did not receive information on the same.

Take medicines: Nearly half (43.1%) of couples in slums received advice on taking medicines on time and 56.9% of them did not receive any advice on the same. On the other hand, 64.4% of rural couples received information and 35.6% of them did not receive any information related to taking medicines on time during their pregnancy.

Heavy household work: In the present study, 42.5% of men from slums advised their wife not to do heavy household work and 57.5% of them did not give advice about the same. Whereas 65% of rural men advised and 35% of them did not advise their wife about not doing heavy household work during pregnancy.

Take more rest: The study revealed that 43.1% of men in slums told their wives about taking more rest during pregnancy and 56.9% of them did not advise them about the same.Likewise, 65.6% of rural men advised and 34.4% of them did not advise them to take more rest during pregnancy.

Intake of nutritional food: Results show that 43.8% of men in slums informed and 56.2% of them did not inform about intake of nutritional food to their pregnant wives. About two- thirds (65.6%) of rural men informed and 34.4% of them did not advise about intake of nutritional food to their wives.

Childbirth at hospital: Data brings out that 38.1% of men in slums talked about the importance of delivery at a hospital to their wives and 61.3% of them did not share the same. Only 0.6% of male from slum did not respond. On the other hand, 65.6% of rural men informed and 34.4% of them did not inform their wives about the importance of childbirth at a hospital.

Importance of breastfeeding: Only 37.5% of men in slums shared and 61.9% of them did not inform their wives about the importance of breastfeeding. Only 0.6% of male from slum did not respond. More than half (60%) of rural men informed their wives about the importance of breastfeeding and 40% of them did not inform them about the same.

Child immunization: In the study, 39.4% of men from slums informed their wives about child immunization and 60.6% of them did not inform them. While 60.6% of rural men informed and 39.4% of them did not inform their wives about child immunization.

Adoption of family planning: Nearly half (47.5%) of men from slum areas informed and 50.6% of them did not inform their wives about adoption of family planning. Only 1.9% of male from slum did not respond. Whereas 64.4% of rural men informed their wives about adoption of family planning and 35.6% of them did not inform them about the same.

Results revealed that there was a area-wise difference in couples' support in physical, economic and informational terms during maternal healthcare. Greater proportion of rural women have received physical, economic and informational support from their husbands towards maternal healthcare in contrast to women in slums.

Case study 3.03: Husband's love more important than money

Radha, now 23 years old, got married when she was only 15 years of age. She delivered her first child at the age of 17 years. She has three children—two sons and a daughter. Her husband is a driver and earns up to 9000 rupees per month.

Though Radha has to make several adjustments in running the family, staying in a slum and trying to meet basic needs, she is very happy. Her husband's love and support is the reason for her happiness even in poverty.

Tender care and concern of her husband especially during pregnancy, his insistence on her consuming a nutritious diet, his help in household work is all Radha could have asked for. Their discussion on family planning helped her go for tubectomy. Open communication between the couple has provided Radha freedom from all sorts of stress and anxiety. Radha feels blessed to have such a loving and caring husband.

Couple's level of satisfaction with physical, economic and informational support

Table no. 3.02: Areaswise distribution of level of couple's satisfaction with physical, economic and informational support in maternal healthcare

Level of satisfaction	*No. of couples*					
	Physical support		*Economic support*		*Informational support*	
	Slum (%)	*Rural (%)*	*Slum (%)*	*Rural (%)*	*Slum (%)*	*Rural (%)*
Yes	150 (93.8%)	159 (99.4%)	150 (93.8%)	159 (99.4%)	83 (51.9%)	110 (68.7%)
No	3 (1.9%)	1 (0.6%)	3 (1.9%)	1 (0.6%)	13 (8.1%)	12 (7.5%)
Other	7 (4.3%)	-	7 (4.3%)	-	48 (30%)	28 (17.5%)
NA/NR/DK	-	-	-	-	16 (10%)	10 (6.3%)
Total	160 (100%)	160 (100%)	160 (100%)	160 (100%)	160 (100%)	160 (100%)

The analysis of table no (3.02) reveals the level of couples' satisfaction about physical, economic and informational support in maternal healthcare. In rural areas, couples reported that they are more satisfied with physical, economic and informational support in maternal healthcare as compared to couples residing in urban slums. Similar proportions of couples from slum and rural areas were satisfied with physical and economic support in maternal healthcare.

Case study 3.04

Unsupportive husband: A big curse

Meena (name changed), 30 years, stays with her husband and three children in a slum in Delhi. Her husband—a driver—has a monthly salary of about 8000 rupees, which in barely sufficient to meet the needs of the family, mainly because her husband spends a big part of it on liquor.

The alcoholic husband is least bothered about the needs and problems of Meena and their children. Illiterate Meena had to struggle a lot during her pregnancy in accessing maternal healthcare services at the health centre as her husband refused to provide any support. Meena had to plead for money to buy medicines prescribed by the doctor from her husband who even asked for bills to confirm whether she had actually bought medicines. Meena terribly missed the tender care of her husband during pregnancy time. She was not given money for extra diet nor did her husband ever discuss her experience of visits for ANC, doctor's advice etc. During delivery, he was absent even though Meena's eyes kept searching for him, although her mother came to provide help. She delivered an underweight child. Unconcerned attitude and behavior of husband has scarred the psyche of Meena, which is difficult to heal.

Perception regarding role of slum and rural husbands in maternal healthcare

In the present study, the researcher also asked the men (husbands) in slum and rural areas about their role in maternal healthcare of their wives. More than a half (57.5%) of husbands from slums and majority (75%) of rural husbands have perceived a role for themselves in the maternal healthcare of their wives. On the other hand, 42.5% of men from slums and only onefourth (25%) of rural husbands did not recognize their role as husband in antenatal, natal and post-natal care of their wives.

Physical support and nutritional support: - In the study, 30% of husbands from slums and 21% of rural husbands reported that they should help in household chores and childcare, accompany wives for ANC visits and child immunization visits and be present at the time of childbirth. They should also look into nutritional needs and be involved in other necessary care of their wives and newborn children.

Emotional/informational/couple communication: - Only 1.2 % of husbands in slums and 8% of rural husbands agreed that they should be responsible for providing informational, emotional support and husband-wife communication required during pregnancy, delivery and after childbirth. It is also helpful for the well-being of women, aiding in easing mental stress related to pregnancy, delivery and the period after childbirth.

Overall husband support: - In slum areas, one-fourth (25%) of husbands and nearly half (46%) of rural husbands revealed that husbands should fulfill all responsibilities in term of physical support (accompany for ANC visits, delivery, child immunization, household, child-care, etc.), nutritional needs, economic support, informational/emotional/ communication during pregnancy, delivery and after childbirth towards their wife and newborn child.

The above discussion revealed that husbands from slum areas emphasize more on physical and nutrition support in their perceived role in maternal healthcare. Likewise, husbands in rural areas more frequently perceived their role and responsibilities in a holistic manner covering emotional/couple communication and physical support during pregnancy, delivery and after delivery. Whereas husbands in slum areas were least concerned about informational/emotional support or couple communication and overall husband-support during maternal healthcare of their wife.

Procedures of measuring couple's views on other aspects/ dimensions of husband- participation in maternal healthcare

Perception on husband support on maternal health care: The twenty two statements have been assigned three-point response categories-'agree', 'disagree' and 'uncertain'. Further, the responses were assigned weightage, '3' to 'agree', '2' to 'uncertain' and '1' to 'disagree' for the positive statements. Whereas, the responses wereassigned weightage, '3' to 'disagree', '2' to 'uncertain' and '1' to 'agree' for the negative statements. The theoretical range is from 12 to 65. This range was divided into two- lower level (12-55) and higher level (56-65). The overall 49.9% of couples have lower level and 50.1% of them have higher level of perception of husband support related to maternal healthcare.

Physical support during maternal healthcare: In the study, the researcher has computed all statements related to physical support provided by couples of both the areas (slum and rural) during and after pregnancy. The responses were assigned weightage, '0' to 'No' and '1' to 'Yes' for the statements. The theoretical range is from 0 to 5. This range is divided into two—lower level (0-3) and higher level (4-5) of physical support. Overall analysis reveals that 57.2% of couples reported lower physical support while 42.8% of them received higher level of physical support in maternal healthcare.

Economic support in maternal healthcare: In the present study, the researcher has computed all statements related to economic support provided by couples during and after pregnancy. The responses were assigned weight, '1' to 'Not required' and '2' to 'Yes' (include conveyance, medicines and extra nutritional food and in the cases where husbands themselves bought medicines, etc.) for the statements. The theoretical range is 1 to 6. This range is divided into two—lower level (1-5) and higher level (6) of economic support. Overall analysis reveals that 55.3% of couples revealed that lower level and 44.7% of women received higher level of economic support in maternal healthcare.

Informational support in maternal healthcare: In the study, the responses of these nine items have been assigned values and summated, and a new composite variable has been generated. The responses were assigned weight, '0' to 'No' and '1' to 'Yes' for the statements. The theoretical and observed score is between 0 to 9. It has two groups— lower level (0-6) and higher level (7-9) of informational support. Overall analysis reveals that 50.3% of couples had lower informational support in maternal healthcare and 49.7% of them have higher level of the same.

Overall husband-participation in maternal healthcare (physical, economic and information support): In the study, the weighted values of these three items (physical support, economic support and informational support) have been summated, and a new composite variable has been generated. It is the overall couple's views related to husband-participation in maternal healthcare. The theoretical range is from 3 to 20. It has two groups: Lower (3-13) and Higher (14-20). Over all analysis reveals that 48.4% of couples got lower husband-participation and more than a half (51.6%) received higher husband-participation in maternal healthcare.

Couple's views and other aspects of husband-participation in maternal healthcare in maternal healthcare

Table no. 3.03: Area-wise distribution of couples and aspects of husband-participation

Aspects ofhusband-participation in maternal healthcare	*No. of couples*	
	Slum (%)	*Rural (%)*
Perception about husband support on maternal healthcare		
Lower level	105 (66.9%)	50 (31.2%)
Higher level	52 (33.1%)	110 (68.8%)
Physical support in maternal healthcare		
Lower level	121 (75.6%)	62 (38.8%)
Higher level	39 (24.4%)	98 (61.2%)
Economic support in maternal healthcare		
Lower level	106 (66.2%)	71 (44.4%)
Higher level	54 (33.8%)	89 (55.6%)
Informational support in maternal healthcare		
Lower level	97 (60.6%)	64 (40%)
Higher level	63 (39.4%)	96 (60%)
Overall husband-participation in maternal healthcare		
Lower level	98 (61.2%)	57 (35.6%)
Higher level	62 (38.8%)	103 (64.4%)

The above table no. (3.03) describes the area-wise details of couples' views on other aspects of husband-participation in maternal healthcare.

Perception of husband support: In the study, couples from rural areas have higher level of perception of husband support in maternal healthcare than their counterparts in urban slums. Results show a strong statistical correlation between locale of couples and perception of husband support on maternal healthcare (Contingency Coefficient = 0.336 and Spearman Correction = 0.356). There is a statistically significant difference between couples residing in slum and rural areas and perception of husband support in maternal healthcare ($\chi2$=40.257, P<0.05).

Physical support: Husbands in rural areas have scored much higher on provision of physical support to their pregnant wives than men in slum areas. There is a strong correlation between locale and level of physical support in maternal healthcare (Contingency Coefficient = 0.349 and Spearman Correlation =0.373). There is significant difference between area-wise couples and level of physical support during maternal healthcare ($\chi2$=44.431, P<0.05). Lower level of physical support by men in slums is a more contributing factor (Standard Residual = +3.1).

Economic support: The analysis of table (no. 3.03) further shows that men from slums have provided lower economic support than those in rural areas. Relevant statistics confirm the same (Contingency Coefficient = 0.215 and Spearman Correlation = 0.220). There is a significant statistical difference between slum and rural couples and level of economic support received from their husband during maternal healthcare ($\chi2$=15.487, P<0.05).

Informational support: Men from rural Delhi have scored higher on informational support and those from slums have figured much lower (see Table 3.03). Results show that rural couples have more informational support as compared to slum couples (Contingency Coefficient = 0.202 and Spearman Correlation= 0.206). Further, there is significant difference between area of couples and level of informational support related to maternal healthcare ($\chi2$=13.613, P<0.05).

Overall husband-participation: The study results, as shown in the table 3.03, show that men from rural areas have higher level of overall husband-participation than their counterparts in slums. Inferential statistics also confirm this (Contingency Coefficient = 0.248 and Spearman Correlation= 0.256). There is a statistically significant difference between women belonging to slum and rural areas and overall level of husband-participation in maternal healthcare ($\chi2$=21.033, P<0.05). Further, men in slums are more contributing factor at lower level of husband-participation in maternal healthcare (Residual Standards = +2.3). On the other hand, rural couples are greater contributing variable at higher level of husband-participation in maternal healthcare (Residual Standards = +2.3).

Case Study 3.05

Being a responsible husband and father

Mahesh (name changed) is a 29 years old graduate. He is a government employee with a monthly salary of 15,000 rupees. He stays in a village in Delhi with his wife and two children. He has been actively involved in providing support to his wife during pregnancy and childbirth. He convincingly stated that a child is the responsibility of both husband and wife; as husband it is my duty to help my wife in every possible way during her pregnancy. He was present with his wife as she delivered their child in the hospital. He kept himself updated with information on pregnancy and childcare and shared the same with his wife. He believes that a child's wellbeing is dependent on mother's emotional state during pregnancy and therefore for family well-being husbands should support their wives.

Couple's views and other aspect of husband-participation in maternal healthcare

Table no. 3.04: Distribution of t test values of couples in slum and rural areas on aspects of husband- participation.

Other aspects of husband-participation in maternal healthcare	*No. of area wise couple's views on husband-participation*					
	Slum		*Rural*		*t test*	*Sig. P<0.05*
	N	*Mean (SD)*	*N*	*Mean (SD)*		
Perception of husband support in maternal healthcare	160	51.26 (10.20)	160	56.82 (6.05)	5.924	.000
Physical support in maternal healthcare	160	2.68 (1.45)	160	3.62 (1.06)	6.584	.000
Economic support in maternal healthcare	160	4.90 (1.07)	160	5.23 (1.03)	2.805	.005
Informational support in maternal healthcare	160	3.73 (4.06)	160	5.69 (4.13)	4.267	.000
Overall husband-participation in maternal healthcare	160	11.32 (4.98)	160	14.55 (4.92)	5.823	.000

The above table no. (3.04) gives details of t test values of locale difference in husband participation in maternal healthcare. There is a statistically significant difference between locale and perception of husband support in maternal healthcare, physical, economic, informational and overall husband-participation in maternal healthcare. Rural men have shown higher scores on various parameters of husband participation: perception of husband support in maternal healthcare, physical, economic, informational and overall husband-participation in maternal healthcare as compared to men from slums.

Area-wise views of men and women on aspects of husband-participation in maternal healthcare

Table no. 3.05 : Area-wise distribution of men and women on aspects of husband-participation.

Other aspects of husband-participation in maternal healthcare	*No. of area-wise men's and women's views on husband-participation*			
	Women		*Husband*	
	Slum	*Rural*	*Slum*	*Rural*
Perception on husband support	**Lower level (%)**	**Higher level (%)**	**Lower level (%)**	**Higher level (%)**
Lower level	56 (70.9%)	23 (29.1%)	50 (61.7%)	31 (38.3%)
Higher level	22 (27.8%)	57 (72.2%)	29 (37.2%)	49 (62.8%)
Physical support in maternal healthcare				
Lower level	57 (64.8%)	31 (35.2%)	32 (74.4%)	11 (25.6%)
Higher level	23 (31.9%)	49 (68.1%)	48 (41%)	69 (59%)
Economic support in maternal healthcare				
Lower level	52 (57.8%)	38 (42.2%)	54 (62.1%)	33 (37.9%)
Higher level	28 (40%)	42 (60%)	26 (35.6%)	47 (64.4%)
Informational support in maternal healthcare				
Lower level	51 (63%)	30 (37%)	47 (58.8%)	33 (41.2%)
Higher level	29 (36.7%)	50 (63.3%)	33 (41.2%)	47 (58.8%)
Overall husband-participation in maternal healthcare				
Lower level	52 65%)	28 (35%)	47 (59.5%)	32 (40.5%)
Higher level	28 (35%)	52 (65%)	33 (40.7%)	48 (59.3%)
Overall satisfaction from husband-participation in maternal healthcare				
Lower level	51 (65.4%)	29 (34.6%)	47 (59.5%)	32 (40.5%)
Higher level	29 (35.4%)	53 (64.4%)	33 (40.7%)	48 (59.3%)

The above table no. (3.05) provides details of area-wise women and husbands' views on other aspects of husband-participation in maternal healthcare.

Perception of husband support: Table 3.05 shows that rural men and women have scored higher on this parameter. The statistics confirm the same (wives'/women's view: Contingency Coefficient = 0.395 and Spearman Correction = 0.430; husbands'/men's views: Contingency Coefficient = 0.238 and Spearman Correlation = 0.245). There is a statistically significant difference between area and respondents' perceptions of husband-support in maternal healthcare (wife: ÷2=29.271, P<0.05; husband: χ2=9.279, P<0.05).

Physical support: As shown in the Table 3.05, among the women stating that their husbands provided higher physical support, the proportion of rural women is more than two times the proportion of women from slums (Contingency Coefficient = 0.310 and Spearman Correlation = 0.327). There is a significant difference between area and women's views on level of physical support received from their husbands during maternal healthcare (χ2=17.071, P<0.05). Further, the ratio of rural and urban males on provision of higher level of physical support is nearly 2:3. Statistics show the same (Contingency Coefficient = 0.284 and Spearman Correlation = 0.296). There is a significant difference between area and husbands' views on level of physical support provided (χ2=14.025, P<0.05).

Economic support: The table 3.05 and relevant statistics (wife's view: Contingency Coefficient = 0.174 and Spearman Correlation = 0.176; husband's view: Contingency Coefficient = 0.255 and Spearman Correlation = 0.264) show no significant difference between area and economic support received and perceived by husband and wife.

Informational support: In the study, rural women have received more informational support as compared to women from slum areas (see Table 3.05). Statistics confirm the same (women's views: Contingency Coefficient = 0.254 and Spearman Correlation= 0.263; men's views: Contingency Coefficient = 0.172 and Spearman Correlation = 0.175). Further, there is a significant difference between area and women's views on level ofinformational support related to maternal healthcare received from their husbands (χ2=11.027, P<0.05).

Overall husband-participation: Higher proportion of rural women have received overall husband participation in contrast to women from slum areas (Table 3.05). Contingency Coefficient = 0.287 and Spearman Correlation= 0.300 confirm the same. There is a statistically significant difference between locale and overall level of husband- participation in maternal healthcare (χ2=14.400, P<0.05).

Quite interestingly, when husbands were asked to rate their level of participation in ante- natal care of their wives, they portrayed themselves more frequently as caring and supportive husbands. Table no. 3.05 provides the details of area-wise distribution of both husbands and wives on husband-participation. When seen in the light of socio-cultural norms, rural areas are taken as more patriarchal than urban areas, and it is a general perception that husbands are more supportive and accommodating in urban areas. However, in the present study these trends are opposite to the popular

Table no. 3.06 : Distribution of t test values of Respondents in slum and rural areas on aspects of husband-participation

Other aspects of husband-participation in maternal healthcare	*No. of location wise women's views on husband-participation*						*No. of location wise men's views on husband-participation*					
	Slum		*Rural*		*t test*	*Sig. P<0.05*	*Slum*		*Rural*		*t test*	*Sig. P<0.05*
	N	*Mean (SD)*	*N*	*Mean (SD)*			*N*	*Mean (SD)*	*N*	*Mean (SD)*		
Perception on husband support	78	51.38 (5.88)	80	57.36 (5.11)	6.815	.000	79	53.10 (8.56)	80	56.63 (5.69)	3.060	.003
Physical support	80	2.78 (1.46)	80	3.63 (1.03)	4.241	.000	80	2.58 (1.44)	80	3.61 (1.09)	4.050	.000
Economic support	80	4.95 (0.99)	80	5.18 (1.04)	1.474	.142	80	4.96 (0.97)	80	5.27 (1.03)	1.971	.050
Informational support	80	3.23 (3.96)	80	5.68 (4.17)	3.804	.000	80	4.12 (4.11)	80	5.70 (4.12)	2.244	.026
Overall husband-participation	80	10.97 (4.80)	80	14.51 (5.00)	4.557	.000	80	8.65 (4.88)	80	11.02 (4.67)	3.140	.002
Overall satisfaction	80	8.10 (1.02)	80	8.66 (0.47)	4.448	.000	80	8.32 (1.20)	80	8.61 (0.99)	1.639	.103
Use of maternal healthcare services	80	4.75 (0.78)	80	5.26 (0.49)	4.923	.000	-	-	-	-	-	-

perception. The reason behind this could be the daily livelihood struggle amidst poverty prevalent in slum areas and as a result husbands may not have time to participate (Contingency Coefficient = 0.184 and Spearman Correlation = 0.188). Results show that there is difference between husbands' stay in slum and rural area and overall level of husband-participation in maternal healthcare ($\chi2=5.626$, $P<0.05$).

Satisfaction from husband-participation: Rural women have recorded higher level of satisfaction from husband-participation than their urban counterparts (Contingency Coefficient = 0.287 and Spearman Correlation = 0.300). The results show that there is a statistically significant difference between area and overall women's satisfaction from husband-participation in maternal healthcare ($\chi2=14.409$, $P<0.05$). Also, rural men are more satisfied with their participation in maternal healthcare than urban men (Contingency Coefficient = 0.168 and Spearman Correlation = 0.170).

Couple's views on husband-participation in maternal healthcare

The above table no. (3.06) provides details of t test values on various aspects of husband participation in maternal healthcare. There is a significant difference with rural women having more positive outlook related to perception of husband-support on maternal healthcare as compared to women from slum areas. Another point to note is that there is also a significant difference between rural and urban women in term of physical support, informational support, overall husband-participation, satisfaction and use of maternal healthcare services. In rural areas, women have received more physical, informational and overall husband-participation; they are more satisfied with husband-participation and have shown better usage of maternal healthcare services as compared to their counterpart women from slum areas. On the other hand, there is no difference between economic support among women staying in slum and rural areas. Hence, the area of women in term of slum and rural areas does not make any difference related to economic support.The t test values of husbands in slum and rural areas: The above table no. (3.06) gives details of t test values of area-wise husband-participation in maternal healthcare. There is a statistically significant difference between area (slum and rural areas) of husbands and perception of husband support on maternal healthcare, physical, economic, informational and overall husband-participation in maternal healthcare. In rural areas, husbands have provided more husband support on maternal healthcare as perceived by them, physical, economic, informational and overall husband-participation in maternal healthcare for their wives as compared to husbands from slum areas. Area of husbands does not make any difference related to husband's satisfaction towards their participation in maternal healthcare, decision-making on household and maternal healthcare.

Thus, the present chapter highlights that men from rural areas have provided more support in maternal healthcare as compared to their counterparts from slums. Rural women got more participation or support from their husbands as compared to slum women. Similarly rural men also showed more participation in maternal healthcare as compared to those in slums. There is also the difference among socio-demographic profile of couples from slum and rural areas. In rural areas, women utilized maternal healthcare services better than slum women. Rural women have received more support during pregnancy and after childbirth.

Chapter - 4

Marital Relation and Utilization of Maternal Healthcare Services

Communication and shared decision-making are critical factors in marital relations and have implications on maternal healthcare. Couple communication related to antenatal care, natal care, after childbirth and family planning issues. One woman shared that '*pati se pregnancy aur delivery ki baatchit karne se bahut-see pareshani dur hoti hai, sath hi achcha lagata hai, kyonki wah bhi samajhte hain.*' (Woman can share her pregnancy and delivery related problems with her husband, it can help in preventing them and also she has a feeling of satisfaction as spouse is empathic). Nowadays, women themselves recognize that sharing maternal healthcare matters with their husbands provides emotional support and satisfaction to women and promotes healthy relation between couples. It helps in resolving various problems as both husband and wife understand each other's situation very well. Communication is the key to resolving any issues related to marital life between couples and is perhaps the most vital aspect in ensuring their mental well-being. Husband-wife communication is essential for women to share their positive and negative feelings, stress and anxiety during pregnancy, during delivery and after delivery. Moreover, husband's concerns provide emotional and mental support to the wife during and after pregnancy. It also creates a sense of responsibility, care and concern among husbands for their wives. "Men see communication as a means of conveying information and demonstrating status, whereas women see it as a means of interacting and establishing emotional ties" (Tannen, 1990; Thorne & Henely, 1975 cited in Fizpatrick & Vangelisti, 1995). Next, one woman mentioned that '*batchit karne se manasik tanaaw kam hoti hai aur pareshani bhi dur ho jati hai.*(Communication helps in overcoming mental stress and problems). Husband-wife communication is most often considered as an important way to help or ensure the husband's participation in maternal healthcare. Several studies have shown that the husband-wife communication on family planning methods is significant. A study by Mishra, et al. (2002) finds that more than three-fourths of the women said they had discussed maternity care and plan for birth with their husbands. About half of the women said they had discussed family planning.

Table no. 4.01: Area-wise distribution of couple communication on maternal healthcare

Statements	*No. of couples*							
	Slum				*Rural*			
	Almost always (%)	*Sometime (%)*	*Almost never (%)*	*NA/DK /NR (%)*	*Almost always (%)*	*Sometime (%)*	*Almost never (%)*	*NA/DK /NR (%)*
Antenatal care								
Pregnancy related feelings	65 (40.6%)	72 (45%)	9 (5.6%)	14 (8.8%)	149 (93.1%)	7 (4.4%)	-	4 (2.5%)
Feel hesitation	3 (1.9%)	13 (8.1%)	129 (80.6%)	15 (9.4%)	2 (1.3%)	4 (2.5%)	150 (93.7%)	4 (2.5%)
Wife comfortable	65 (40.6%)	70 (43.8%)	11 (6.8%)	14 (8.8%)	149 (93.1%)	7 (4.4%)	-	4 (2.5%)
Husband talks kindly	94 (58.8%)	46 (28.7%)	8 (5%)	12 (7.5%)	149 (93.1%)	5 (3.1%)	2 (1.3%)	4 (2.5%)
Husband talks gently	93 (58.1%)	43 (26.9%)	12 (7.5%)	12 (7.5%)	147 (91.9%)	7 (4.4%)	2 (1.2%)	4 (2.5%)
Natal care								
Delivery-related problems	45 (28.1%)	75 (46.9%)	24 (15%)	16 (10%)	134 (83.8%)	15 (9.3%)	7 (4.4%)	(2.5%)
Delivery-related feeling	45 (28.1%)	71 (44.4%)	31 (19.4%)	13 (8.1%)	134 (83.8%)	20 (12.5%)	2 (1.2%)	4 (2.5%)
Post natal care								
Newborn child's health	44 (27.5%)	81 (50.6%)	23 (14.4%)	12 (7.5%)	133 (83.1%)	16 (10%)	7 (4.4%)	4 (2.5%)
Problems emerging after childbirth	40 (25%)	90 (56.3%)	18 (11.2%)	12 (7.5%)	132 (82.5%)	23 (14.4%)	1 (0.6%)	4 (2.5%)
Interest in post natal care	84 (52.5%)	53 (33.1%)	10 (6.3%)	13 (8.1%)	142 (88.8%)	12 (7.5%)	2 (1.2%)	4 (2.5%)
Family planning								
Talk about family planning	14 (8.8%)	41 (25.6%)	23 (14.4%)	82 (51.2%)	61 (38.1%)	18 (11.2%)	3 (1.9%)	78 (48.8%)
Nervous to discuss	-	8 (5%)	65 (40.6%)	87 (54.4%)	2 (1.2%)	-	80 (50%)	78 (48.8%)
Husband share particular method	12 (7.5%)	38 (23.8%)	25 (15.6%)	85 (53.1%)	17 (10.6%)	29 (18.1%)	36 (22.5%)	78 (48.8%)
Husband become aggressive	1 (0.6%)	5 (3.1%)	67 (41.9%)	87 (54.4%)	-	3 (1.9%)	79 (49.3%)	78 (48.8%)
Husband takes interest	30 (18.8%)	40 (25%)	5 (3.1%)	85 (53.1%)	74 (46.2%)	8 (5%)	-	78 (48.8%)

The present chapter looks into couple communication on maternal healthcare, decision- making on household and maternal healthcare as well as role of husband in household work during and after pregnancy.

Couple communication on maternal healthcare

Table no.4.01 presents the details of couple communication related to maternal healthcare among slum and rural husband-wife. Most of the couples from rural areas take more interest and communicate about antenatal care, natal care, post-natal care and family planning as compared to couples residing in slum areas. It seems that in slums and resettlement colonies, people are hard-pressed with livelihood issues and struck in economic impoverishment. Consequently they may not have enough time and inclination to communicate and share moments of parenthood.

Antenatal care: In the study, 40.6% of couples in slums almost always shared pregnancy- related feelings. Most (93.1%) of the rural couples almost always shared about pregnancy- related feelings. On the other hand, 8.1% of couples in slums sometimes hesitate to communicate about pregnancy-related feelings. Only 2.5% of rural couples sometimes hesitate to communicate about pregnancy-related feelings. Further, 40.6% of couples in slums cited that the wife almost always is comfortable and 93.1% of rural couples reported that their wife is almost always comfortable to share pregnancy-related feelings. Likewise, more than a half (58.8%) of men from slums and most (93.1%) of rural men almost always talk kindly with their wives during pregnancy.Natal care: The present study revealed that 28.1% of couples from slums almost always shared delivery-related problems and feelings related to childbirth, whereas 83.8% of rural couples almost always shared the same.

Post-natal care: Further, more than one fourth (27.5%) of couples from slums reported that they almost always shared thoughts about their newborn child's health after delivery. Majority (83.1%) of rural couples mentioned that they almost always discussed their newborn child's health after delivery. One fourth (25%) of couples in slums almost always discussed health problems after childbirth whereas 82.5% of rural couples almost always talked about health problems after childbirth. More than half (52.5%) of couples from slums almost always take interest in discussion on post-natal care. Most (88.8%) of rural couples almost always take interest in discussions related to post-natal care.

Family Planning: In the study, 8.8% of couples from slums almost always shared thoughts about family planning. Likewise, 38.1% of rural couples almost always discussed family planning. Further, 40.6% of couples from slums almost never feel nervous to talk about family planning. Half

(50%) of rural couples almost never feel nervous to discuss family planning. On the other hand, 23.8% of couples from slums sometimes talk about particular methods of family planning. Only 18.1% of rural couples sometime shared about particular methods of family planning. Next, 3.1% of women in slums reported that husbands sometime became aggressive during discussions on family planning. Only 1.9% of rural women cited that husbands sometime became aggressive during discussions on family planning. Another, 18.8% of women in slums mentioned that husbands almost always take interest in family planning discussions. Nearly half (46.2%) of rural women reported that husband almost always take interest in family planning discussions.

Case study 4.01

Mother-in-law- A solace

Rekha (name changed) a young 22 years old woman came to Delhi a few years ago with her mother-in-law and husband. Her husband works in a private company and earns about 8000 rupees per month.

Rekha had dreamt of a loving and caring life partner as most girls do. Married at the age of 17 years, she found a wide gap between her dreams and reality. Her alcoholic husband is unconcerned towards her tender feelings.

Rekha, a mother of two children never wanted a third child but she couldn't gather courage to put her foot down against the wishes of her husband. She, however, received proper care and attention from her mother-in-law. Rekha affirms that she is uncomfortable to talk to her husband on matters related to maternal healthcare but with her 'sasu-ma', she can freely do so. Her mother-in-law provided all the support during her pregnancy and after childbirth. Despite that, she delivered an underweight child. Has her husband's lack of support taken a toll on her maternal health?

Area-wise couple's views on decision-making on household matters and maternal healthcare

Daily menu of food: In the study, 15% of couples in slums mentioned that the wife takes decisions, followed by husbands (32.5%), joint (19.4%) and other (33.1%) about daily menu of food. On the other hand, in 2.5% cases wives, 20% husbands, 20.6% jointly and 56.9% cases other family members have a say in daily menu of food as cited by rural couples.

Purchasing groceries items: In only 10% cases wives, 35% husbands, 18.1% joint and 36.9% cases other family members take decisions on purchasing groceries items as mentioned by couples from slums. Whereas in rural cases it was 1.3% wives, 20.6% husbands, 22.5% joint and 55.6% other family members took decisions related to purchasing groceries items.

Purchasing major household items like TV., jewelry, etc: The present study revealed that in 8.8% cases wives, husbands in 35.6% cases, joint in 20.6% cases and in 35% other family members have a say in matters related to purchasing major household items like TV., jewelry , etc. as cited by couples from slums. Likewise, rural couples reported that 21.3% of husbands, 23.1% joint and 55.6% of other family members take decisions related to purchasing major household item like TV., jewelry, etc. It seems that women did not have much say in purchasing of major household items in rural areas.

Children's schooling: The couples from slum areas reported that in 8.8% cases wives, in 35% husbands, in 25% joint and in 31.2% cases other family members take decisions related to children's schooling. While 1.3% of rural couples revealed that their wives, 23.1% said husbands, 23.1% said joint and 52.5% said other family members have a say in matters related to children's schooling.

Purchasing clothes for child, herself, etc.: Results show that in 11.2% cases wives, 33.1% cases husbands, 21.9% cases joint and 33.8% cases family members have a say in matters related to purchasing clothes for child, herself, etc., as shared by couples from slums. On the other hand, in 1.9% cases wives, 21.2% cases husbands, 23.1% cases joint and 53.8% cases other family members take decisions on purchasing clothes for child and mother among rural couples.

Purchasing property or land: In slum areas, 4.4% cases had wives, 36.2% had husbands, 21.8% had joint and 37.5% had other family members take decisions related to purchasing property or land. Further, in 23.8% cases husbands, in 21.2% cases joint and in 55% cases other family members take decisions on purchasing property or land among rural couples. In rural areas women did not have much of a say in matters related to purchasing of property or land.

Children's health: In the present study, 9.4% cases had wives, 33.7% cases had husbands, 23.8% had joint and 33.1% had other family members getting a say in matters related to children's health problems as cited by couples in slums. Whereas only one (0.6%) wife, in 22.5% cases husbands, in 23.8% cases joint and in 53.1% cases other family members have a say in matters related to children's health problems among rural couples.

Decision-making on maternal healthcare

Visiting health centre for ANC: In the present study, in 6.9% cases wives, in 41.2% cases husbands, in 26.3% cases joint and in 25.2% cases other family members take decisions related to visiting health centres for antenatal check-ups among couples from slums. Whereas only one (0.6%) wife, 26.3% cases had husbands, 33.1% cases had joint and 40% cases had other family members take decisions about visiting health centres for antenatal check-ups as cited by rural couples.Purchasing medicine for own health: Only in 5.6% cases the wives, in 43.8% cases the husbands, in 25% cases joint and in 24.4% cases other family members take decisions about purchasing medicines for their own health as mentioned by couples in slums. Only 1.2 percent of couples from slum did not provide money for purchasing medicines for their own health. On the other hand, in 1.2% cases wives, in 25.6% cases husbands, in 33.8% cases joint and in 39.4% cases other family members take decisions related to purchase of medicines for own health among rural couples.

Spending money on ultrasound scans: Results show that in 5% cases wives, in 37.5% cases husbands, in 26.3% cases joint and in 25.6% cases other family members take decisions related to spending money on ultrasound scans among couples from slums. Only in 5.6% cases women from slums did not have ultrasound scans due to low income. Likewise, in 1.9% cases wives, in 27.5% cases husbands, in 31.2% cases joint and in 39.4% cases other family members take decisions about spending money on ultrasound scans among rural couples.

Spending money on desired food during pregnancy: The present study revealed that in 11.2% cases wives, in 40.6% cases husbands, in 23.8% cases joint and in 24.4% cases other family members have a say in matters related to spending money on desired food during pregnancy as mentioned by couples in slums. Further, in 2.5% cases wives, in 26.3% cases husbands, in 30.6% cases joint and in 40.6% cases other family members take decisions on spending money on desired food during pregnancy as cited by rural couples.

Visiting family relatives' homes: The couples in slums reported that in 4.4% cases wives, in 45.6% cases husbands, in 25.6% cases joint and in 24.4% cases other family members take decisions about visiting family relatives' homes during pregnancy. Only two (1.2%) of wife, in 26.3% cases husbands, in 30.6% cases joint and in 41.9% cases other family members have a say in matters related to visiting family relatives' homes during pregnancy as mentioned by rural couples.

Visiting health centre for pregnancy-related problems: The study revealed that in 6.9% cases wives, in 40.6% cases husbands, in 27.5% cases joint and in 25% cases other family members take decision about visiting health centers for pregnancy-related problems as cited by couples from slums. Likewise, two (1.2%) of the wives, in 27.5% cases husbands, in38.8% cases joint and in 37.5% cases other family members take decisions about visiting health centers for pregnancy-related problems among rural couples.

Place of delivery: Only in 6.2% cases wives, in 40% cases husbands, in 30% cases joint and in 23.8% cases other family members take decisions about place of childbirth among couples from slums. Whereas three (1.9%) of the wives, in 29.4% cases husbands, in 31.2% cases joint and in 37.5% cases other family members take decisions on place of delivery among rural couples.

Visiting health centers for common health-problems after delivery: Findings of the study reveal that in slum areas in 8.1% of cases wives, in 41.3% cases husbands, in 25.6% cases joint and in one fourth (25%) cases other family members have a say in matters related to visiting health centers for common health problem after delivery. Next, in rural areas in 1.9% cases wives, in 28.7% cases husbands, in 30.6% cases joint and in 38.8% cases other family members take decisions about visiting health centers for common health problems after childbirth.

Immunization of children: Results show that in 8.1% cases wives, in 40% cases husbands, in 25.6% cases joint and in 26.3% cases other family members take decisions on immunization of children among couples from slums. On the other hand, in rural areas in 1.9% cases wives, in 28.8% cases husbands, in 31.2% cases joint and in 38.1% cases other family members have a say in matters related to immunization of children.

Adopting Family planning methods: In slum areas, only in 4.4% cases wives, in 23.8% cases husbands, in 49.4% cases joint and in 19.4% cases other family members take decisions related to adopting of methods of family planning. However, 3% of couples from slum did not take any decision because of religious obligation. On the other hand, in 2.5% cases wives, in 8.1% cases husbands, in 76.9% cases joint and in 11.9% cases other family members take decisions on adopting family planning methods in the rural setting. Only 0.6% of husband from rural did not respond.

Overall findings reveal slum and rural area-wise couples' decision-making related to household matters and maternal healthcare. In rural areas, most couples mentioned that husbands and other family members (such as father-in-laws, mother-in-laws, familyrelatives, etc.) were main decision-makers related to household matters. In maternal healthcare decision-making, most of the couples from slums reported that husbands have more say as compared to women. Further, couples from slums revealed that women have more decision-making powers related to household chores and maternal healthcare as compared to rural women. On the other hand, rural couples mentioned that other family members have more say in household matters. When it comes to decision-making on maternal healthcare most of the rural couples have taken joint decisions. In rural areas, it seems that couples have positive stance in terms of recognizing that maternal healthcare is the responsibility of both husband and wife.

Case study 4.02

No control over my own life?

Rashmi (name changed) could study up to 10th standard, got married when she was only 17 years and came to Delhi from Bihar. Presently, she lives in the slums of Delhi in a joint family with her in-laws. Her husband is the only earning member and with his monthly income of 9000 rupees, Rashmi had to compromise on nutritional food and other wishes during pregnancy.

However, what hurts Rashmi the most is lack of communication with husband. He is often rude and insensitive toward her, which discourages Rashmi even to discuss important matters related to birth spacing and pregnancy with him.

Rashmi has to be a doting *bahu* who without any questions follows commands of her mother-in-law and husband, as they take all the decisions in the family from menu for lunch/dinner to planning children.

Rashmi who became a mother when she had just turned 19 years, wanted to have spacing of at least two years, but in the family her wishes have no value.

Area Wise Husband-participation in Various Activities during Pregnancy and After Pregnancy

Brings the Medicines: Little less than a half (47.5%) of husbands in urban slums, most of the time, brought medicines for their wives during pregnancy. Another, 28.7% of men from slums occasionally brought medicines and only 18.8% of them never brought medicines. Rest (5%) of the husbands from slums were in not applicable category. Almost two-thirds (65%) of rural husbands most of time brought medicines for their wives during pregnancy. Only 22.5% of rural men occasionally brought and 7.5% of them never brought medicinesfor their wives. Rest (5%) of husbands were in not applicable category.

Take Care for Nutritional Food Intake: More than a half (52.5%) of husbands from slums most of the time did take care of the nutritional food intake of their wives. Next, 37.5% of them occasionally took care and only ten percent of them never took care of the nutritional food intake of their wives. Results show that 53.8% of rural husbands most of the time did take care of the nutritional food intake of their wives. Next, 38.7% of rural husbands occasionally took care of it and only 7.5% of rural husbands never took care of the nutritional food intake of their wives.

Fetch Drinking Water From Outside: Data brings out that 46.3% of husbands from slums most of the time did fetch drinking water from outside the home during their wives' pregnancy. On the other hand, 26.2% of husbands in slums occasionally fetched drinking water from outside the home during their wives' pregnancy. Only 17.5% of husbands in slums never fetched drinking water from outside the home during their wives' pregnancy. Rest (10%) of husbands in slums were in not applicable category. Data brings out that 16.2% of rural husbands most of the time and 18.8% of them occasionally did fetch drinking water from outside the home during their wives' pregnancy. Only 6.2% of husbands never fetched drinking water from outside the home during their wives' pregnancy. Rest (58.8%) of them were in not applicable category.

Bring the Grocery (Ration): Results show that 42.5% of husbands from slums most of the time did bring groceries (ration) during pregnancy of their wives. Further 37.5% of husbands from slums occasionally purchased groceries and only 20% of them never brought groceries during pregnancy of their wives. Half (50%) of rural husbands most of the time and 31.2% of them occasionally purchased groceries during pregnancy of their wives. Only 18.8% of rural husbands never bought groceries during pregnancy of their wives.

Cooking the Meal: More than half (62.5%) of husbands from slums never cooked meals during their wives' pregnancy. On the other hand, 37.5% of husbands from slums occasionally cooked meals during pregnancy of their wives. Majority (77.5%) of rural husbands never cooked meals during their wives' pregnancy. Only 22.5% of rural husbands occasionally cooked meals during their wives' pregnancy.

Making the Tea or Coffee: In the study, 58.8% of husbands from slums never made tea or coffee for their pregnant wives whereas 41.2% of them occasionally prepared tea or coffeefor them. More than half (73.8%) of rural husbands never made tea or coffee for their pregnant wives. On the other hand, 26.2% of rural husbands occasionally made tea or coffee for them.

Cleaning the Home: One fourth (25%) of husbands from slums occasionally cleaned house during their wives' pregnancy, while three fourths (75%) never cleaned the house. In rural areas, 23.8% of husbands occasionally cleaned the house during their wives' pregnancy and 76.2% of them never did so.

Washing Clothes: Almost two-thirds (67.5%) of husbands from slums never washed clothes. Further, 31.3% of them occasionally washed clothes during and after delivery. Only one (1.2%) man from the slums washed clothes most of the time. In the present study, 72.5% of rural husbands never washed clothes. Next, 27.5% of rural husbands occasionally washed clothes during and after delivery.

Feeding the New Born Child: Results show that 72.5% of husbands from slums occasionally fed newborn children bottle-milk and 25% of them never fed newborns. Rest (2.5%) of them were in not applicable category. Findings show that 63.8% of rural husbands occasionally and 32.5% of them never fed newborn children bottle-milk. Rest (3.7%) of them were in not applicable category.

Changing Nappies of Child: Majority (70%) of husbands in slums occasionally changed nappies of their children and 30% of them never did so. Majority (72.5%) of rural husbands occasionally changed nappies of their children and only one (1.3%) man changed nappies of his child most of the time. Further, 26.2% of them never did so.

Cleaning the newborn: Most (86.2%) husbands from slums occasionally cleaned their newborns and 13.8% of them never did so. In rural areas, 85% of husbands occasionally cleaned their newborns and 13.7% of them never did so. Only one (1.3%) man from rural setting did the same most of the time.

Cleaning Utensils: The findings show that 70% of husbands in slums never cleaned utensils during pregnancy and after delivery of their wives. Next, 28.8% of husbands occasionally did so. Only one (1.2%) man was in not applicable category. Data brings out that 77.5% of rural husbands never cleaned utensils during pregnancy and after delivery of their wives. On the other hand, 22.5% of rural husbands occasionally cleaned utensils during the same.

Helping in Heavy Work: About two-thirds (68.8%) of husbands from slums occasionally helped in heavy household work during pregnancy of their wives and only 2.5% of them helped most of the time in heavy household work. Further, 28.7% of husbands from slums never helped in heavy household work. Majority (87.5%) of rural husbands occasionally helped in heavy household work during pregnancy of their wives and only 11.2% of them never helped in the same. Rest (1.3%) of the husband was in not applicable category.

Dropping Child to School: Findings show that in slum areas, 7.5% men most of the time and 13.8% men occasionally dropped their children to school during and after pregnancy of their wives. 16.2% of them never dropped the children to school. Rest (62.5%) of the men were in not applicable category. Likewise, 12.5% of rural husbands most of the time and 17.5% of them occasionally dropped their children to school during and after pregnancy of their wives, and 11.2% of them never dropped their children to school. Rest (58.8%) of the rural husbands were in not applicable category.

Tending Crying Newborn: Results show that in slum areas, 3.7% of husbands most of the time and 93.8% occasionally tended their crying newborn and 2.5% of them never tended their crying newborn. Majority (91.2%) of rural husbands occasionally tended their crying newborn and only one (1.3%) rural man most of the time tended his crying newborn. Next, 7.5% of fathers never managed their crying newborn.

Escorting Child from School: An equal proportion (3.7% each) of husbands from slums most of the time and occasionally escorted their children back home from school during and after pregnancy of their wives whereas 26.3% of fathers never escorted their children back from school. Rest (66.3%) of men from slums were in not applicable category. In the study, 8.7% of rural fathers most of the time and 12.5% of them occasionally escorted their children from school during and after pregnancy of their wives, while 20% of rural fathers never escorted their children back from school during and after pregnancy of their wives. Rest (58.8%) of the rural men were in not applicable category.

Procedures of measuring couple's views on communication and decision-making on household and maternal healthcare

Communication between Husbands and Wives on Maternal Healthcare: There were fifteen statements in which twelve were positive and three were negative statements. Further, the responses were assigned weight, '3' to 'almost always', '2' to 'sometimes' and '1' to 'almost never ' for the positive statements. Whereas, the responses were assigned weight, '3' to 'almost never', '2' to 'sometime' and '1' to 'almost always' for the negative statements. The theoretical range is from 8 to 45. This is divided into two groups: lower level (8-30) and higher level (31-45). Overall analysis reveals that more than a-half (53.4 %) of couples have lower level of husband-wife communication and 46.6% of them have higher level of husband-wife communication on maternal healthcare.

Decision-making on household matters: In the study, the weighted values of these seven items have been summated, and a new composite variable has been generated. These statements have been assigned four-point response categories-'wife', 'husband', 'joint' and 'other'. Further, the responses were assigned weight, '4' to 'joint', '3' to 'wife', '2' to 'husband' and '1' to 'others' for the statements. The theoretical range is from 7 to 28. This is divided into two groups: lower level (7-12) and higher level (14-28). Over all analysis reveals that 44.7% of couples have lower level of decision-making and 55.3% of them have higher level of decision-making on household matters.

Decision-making on maternal healthcare matters: In the study, responses of weighted values of these ten items have been summated, and a new composite variable has been generated. These statements have been assigned four-point response categories-'wife', 'husband', 'joint' and 'other'. Further, the responses were assigned weight, '4' to 'joint', '3' to 'wife', '2' to 'husband' and '1' to 'others' for the positive statements. The theoretical range is from 9 to 40. This is divided into two - lower level (9-19) and higher level (20-40). Overall analysis reveals that 44.4% of couples have lower level of decision- making whereas 55.6% of them have higher level of decision-making on maternal healthcare.

Table no. 4. 02 : Area-wise distribution of couples and aspects of husband-participation

Aspects of husband-participation in maternal healthcare	*No. of couples*	
	Slum (%)	*Rural (%)*
Couple Communication on maternal healthcare		
Decision-making on household matters		
Lower level	56 (35%)	87 (54.4%)
Higher level	104 (65%)	73 (45.6%)
Decision-making on maternal healthcare		
Lower level	63 (39.4%)	79 (49.4%)
Higher level	97 (60.6%)	81 (50.6%)

The above table no. (4.02) describes the area-wise details of couples' views on other aspects of husband-participation in maternal healthcare.

Couple communication: In the study, couples from slums have more frequently a lower level of couple communication while those from rural areas have higher. There is no significant difference between locale and couple communication related to maternal healthcare ($\chi 2$=2.111, P>0.05).

Decision-making on household: Interestingly, couples from slums figure higher on joint decision-making than those in rural areas (also see: Contingency Coefficient = 0.191 and Spearman Correlation = -0.195). There is a significant difference between area of couples and decision-making on household matters ($\chi 2=12.150$, $P<0.05$).

Decision-making on maternal healthcare: A higher proportion of couples from slums have joint decision-making on issues related to maternal healthcare (Contingency Coefficient = 0.062 and Spearman Correlation = 0.063). There is no difference between locale of couples and decision-making on maternal healthcare ($\chi 2=1.251$, $P>0.05$). This may be because of the presence of a higher proportion of nuclear families in urban slums than rural Delhi.

Case study 4.03

Patriarchal mind set: Hurdle to husband participation

Ram (name changed) a thirty-five-year-old shopkeeper stays with his wife, two daughters and mother in a village of Delhi. Though he extends help to his pregnant wife in escorting her to the doctor for antenatal check-ups, his patriarchal notions still dominate. "*Pati ko ghar ke kaamkaaj mein madad nahi karni chahiye kyonki agar madad karte hein toh bachche ka janm operation se hota hai. Patni yadi zyada kaam kare toh bachche ka janm aaraam se ho jata hai*" (Husband should not help his wife in household work because if hedoes so, wife will have delivery through Caesarean section/ operation. If wife works a lot, she will deliver the child with ease through normal delivery.) – commented Ram. This justification by him reflects his patriarchal mind set. To him, his role as husband is confined to providing economic support and if needed, to arrange for her doctor's visits. He does not believe in sharing feelings with wife on a child's entry into their life and does not feel the need to know pregnancy-related problems of his wife, for which, according to him, there is his mother.

Couple's views and other aspects of husband-participation in maternal healthcare

The above table no. (4.03) gives details of t test values of locale difference in husband- participation in maternal healthcare. There is a statistically significant difference between locale and couple communication. On the other hand, there is no difference between decision-making on maternal healthcare whether couples belong to slum or rural areas.

Table no. 4.03: Distribution of t test values of couples in slum and rural areas on aspects of husband-participation in maternal healthcare.

Other aspects of husband-participation in maternal healthcare	*No. of area-wise couple's views on husband-participation*					
	Slum		*Rural*		*t test*	*Sig. P<0.05*
	N	*Mean (SD)*	*N*	*Mean (SD)*		
Couple Communication on maternal healthcare	151	28.98 (8.69)	158	35.46 (7.70)	6.943	.000
Decision-making on household matters	160	15.28 (7.51)	160	13.40 (8.25)	-2.132	.034
Decision-making on maternal healthcare	160	23.65 (10.30)	160	23.73 (11.70)	0.061	.952

Area-wise views of men and women on aspects of husband-participation in maternal healthcare

Table no. 4.04: Area-wise distribution of men and women on aspects of husband-participation

Other aspectsof husband-participation in maternal healthcare	*No. of area-wise men's and women's views on husband-Participation*			
	Women		*Men*	
	Slum	*Rural*	*Slum*	*Rural*
Couple Communication on maternal healthcare	**Lower level (%)**	**Higher level (%)**	**Lower level (%)**	**Higher level (%)**
Lower level	47 (54.7%)	39 (45.3%)	40 (50.6%)	39 (49.4%)
Higher level	31 (43.1%)	41 (56.9%)	33 (45.8%)	39 (54.2%)
Decision-making on household				
Lower level	28 (38.9%)	44 (61.1%)	28 (39.4%)	43 (60.6%)
Higher level	52 (59.1%)	36 (40.9%)	52 (58.4%)	37 (41.6%)
Decision-making on maternal healthcare				
Lower level	39 (50.6%)	38 (49.4%)	46 (53.5%)	40 (46.5%)
Higher level	41 (49.4%)	42 (50.6%)	34 (45.9%)	40 (54.1%)

The above table no. (4.04) provides details of area-wise women's and husbands' views on other aspects of husband-participation in maternal healthcare.

Couple communication: In the study, one woman from rural area said that "*pregnancy problems mai apni saas se batati thi. kyoki jyada pata hai ve to aurato ki baaten hoti hai*" (I always shared pregnancy problems with my mother-in-law because she knew more and it is women's domain). Seemingly, area has no differential impact on couple communication and

Table no. 4. 05 : Distribution of t test values of respondents in slum and rural areas on aspects of husband-participation

Other aspects of husband-participation in maternal healthcare	*No. of location wise women's views on husband-participation*						**No. of location wise men's views on husband-participation**					
	Slum		*Rural*		**t test**	**Sig. P<0.05**	**Slum**		**Rural**		*t test*	*Sig. P<0.05*
	N	*Mean (SD)*	*N*	*Mean (SD)*			**N**	**Mean (SD)**	**N**	**Mean (SD)**		
Couple Communication	78	28.55 (9.02)	80	35.53 (7.65)	5.250	.000	73	29.45 (8.35)	78	35.39 (7.80)	4.521	.000
Decision-making on household	80	15.52 (7.70)	80	13.57 (8.44)	-1.525	.129	80	15.03 (7.35)	80	13.22 (8.10)	-1.481	.141
Decision-making on maternal healthcare	80	24.52 (9.39)	80	24.61 (10.85)	0.055	.957	80	22.78 (10.15)	80	22.81 (11.39)	0.015	.988

the statistics confirm this (wife's views: Contingency Coefficient = 0.115 and Spearman Correlation = 0.116; husband's views: Spearman Correlation = 0.048).

Gender Differentials on decision-making on household matters: In the study, more than a half (59.1%) of slum women have higher level and while 61.1% of rural women have lower level of decision-making on household activities (Contingency Coefficient = 0.190 and Spearman Correlation = -0.201). There is a difference between area and women's decision-making on household matters ($\chi 2=6.465$, $P<0.05$). In rural areas, 41.6 of husbands have lower level and 39.4% of husbands from slums have lower level of decision-making on household matters. Results show that couples from slum areasmore frequently make decisions collectively in contrast to rural couples (Contingency Coefficient = 0.185 and Spearman Correlation = -0.189).

Gender differentials on decision-making on maternal healthcare: Results show that there is no significant difference between whether women belong to slum or rural areas and overall decision-making on maternal healthcare (Contingency Coefficient = 0.013 and Spearman Correlation = 0.013; $\chi 2=0.025$, $P>0.05$). Further, more than a half (53.5%) of men from slums have lower level of decision-making related to maternal healthcare and 54% of husbands from rural areas have higher level on the same. (Contingency Coefficient = 0.075 and Spearman Correlation = 0.075). There is no significant difference between area-wise husbands' responses and decision-making on maternal healthcare ($\chi 2=0.905$, $P>0.05$).

Couple's views on husband-participation in maternal healthcare

The above table no. (4.05) provides details of t test values on various aspects of husband participation in maternal healthcare. There is a statistically significant difference between area of women and level of couple communication on maternal healthcare. Women from rural areas more frequently communicate/share matters related to maternal healthcare with their husbands as compared to slum women, who have less couple communication on the same. On the other hand, there is no difference between decision-making related to household and maternal healthcare among women staying in slum and rural areas. The area of women in terms of slum and rural areas does not make any difference to decision- making on household matters and maternal healthcare.

The t test values of husbands in slum and rural areas: The above table no. (4.05) gives details of t test values of area-wise husband participation in maternal healthcare. There is a statistically significant difference between area (slum and rural areas) of couple communication.

In rural areas, husbands have provided more husband support on maternal healthcare as perceived by them, and have better couple communication in maternal healthcare compared to husbands from slum areas. On the other hand, there is no locale difference between decision-making related to household and maternal healthcare, whether they reside in slum or rural areas. The area of husbands does not make any difference related to decision-making on household matters and maternal healthcare.

Case study 4.04

Supportive Husband: A blessing

Sanjeev (name changed), 27 years old, runs a petty business. Having migrated from Uttar Pradesh a few years back, he now lives in a slum with his wife and two daughters. He has studied up to Xth while his wife is illiterate. Sanjeev's life is full of suffering and challenges. Polio claimed his limb at a very early age. In Delhi, he is able to earn barely 4000 rupees a month and many expenses are held up for want of money.

However, the struggle for livelihood has not made Sanjeev emotionally hardened. His wife considers herself very lucky as he accompanied her to the health centre when she was pregnant. He helps in household work, takes care of the children and even cooks food when his wife is not feeling well. He has discussed in detail about the food to be eaten during pregnancy, taking rest, remaining happy and calm. He would encourage his wife to share her pregnancy-related feelings and apprehensions.

Though on the birth of his second daughter, his relatives frowned upon the news, Sanjeev welcomed the new life with open arms and elation.

With Sanjeev's love and support, his wife and daughters feel secure,confident and happy.

Thus, the present chapter highlights that men from rural areas have more communication about maternal healthcare as compared to their counterparts from slums. The area (slum and rural areas) of women and their husbands or couples is also affecting their participation in maternal healthcare, communication, decision-making and so on.

Chapter - 5

Conclusions & Suggestions

Maternal health is an important indicator of social development. Rise in maternal mortality rate directly influences the infant mortality rate. According to Beijing Declaration and the Platform for Action (Fourth Conference), "Women's health involves their emotional, social and physical well-being and is determined by the social, political and economic context of their lives, as well as by biology" (1996). There are many challenges faced by women during the maternal period and there is a serious question before us as to how we are going to address their issues. In the world, every day 830 women die from pregnancy- related complications (WHO, 2016). In India, one woman dies every 5 minutes due to pregnancy and childbirth-related problems (The Times of India, 2016). The struggles women have to face are not only at physiological but also at the psychological and social levels. Being vulnerable, majority of the women in Indian society are unable to enjoy basic rights like right to health, right to survival and so on.

Investment in safe motherhood (maternal health) improves a woman's health and child's health. Maternal health is the essence of healthy families and a healthy society. The implication of maternal mortality and the complications it causes for the health of infants and older children are quite serious.

Husband-participation in maternal healthcare is an essential component to ensure proper utilization of maternal healthcare services. Positive perception of husband support on maternal healthcare, healthy couple-communication, joint decision-making related to household matters and maternal healthcare lead to healthier mothers and newborn children.

The present study has looked into the usage of maternal healthcare services, factors that influence maternal health among women, husband-participation in physical support (refers to accompanying for ANC visits, b eing present at the time of delivery, accompanying for child immunization, helping in household work and help in caring for older children), economic support (includes money for travel expenses, money for medical check-ups and medicines and extra money for nutritional food intake) and informational support (refers to ANC visits, intake of medicines, proper rest, institutional delivery, breast- feeding , etc.), perception of husband-support in maternal healthcare, husband-wife communication related to maternal healthcare, decision-making on household matters and maternal healthcare, role perceived by men as husbands in maternal healthcare, child milestone development and linkage with socio-demographic aspects, intra-family, extra- family factors such as education of women and husbands, age at marriage of respondents, type of house, occupation of husbands, monthly income of husbands, religion and so on. The study also does comparative analysis of rural and urban (slums) locale respondents' usage of maternal healthcare services and various aspects of husband-participation. To gather a comprehensive understanding about women and their husbands' views and overall area-wise couples' views, attention has been paid to both quantitative data analysis and qualitative insight into their situation. In light of the objectives of the present study, information has been collected from 160 women and 160 men (their husbands). It includes 80 couples from slums (combined JJ camp Rakhi market, Zakhir and Navjeevan and Nehru camp, Govindpuri, Kalkaji) and 80 couples from rural areas (combined Holmabi Kalan and Dichaon Kalan) of Delhi.

Age is a crucial variable to understand child-bearing and rearing practices and challenges among women. Area-wise findings show that in slums there was a greater proportion of young women (18 to 24 years= 56.3%) than those (31.3%) in rural areas. Among men, 61.3% from slums and 77.5% from rural areas were in the age bracket of 25-34 years. Rural couples were more literate and educated than those in urban slums. Women predominantly had been housewives, there were more working women from rural areas than urban slums.

Further, men from slum areas were frequently engaged in low paying semi-skilled or unskilled jobs while in rural Delhi, men were often in government jobs or engaged in their own business.

Men's monthly income range was from Rs. 3000 to 50000 with mean monthly income being Rs. 9973.82. Nearly 51.9 % men had monthly income below 10,000 rupees. Men with higher monthly income were able to frequently provide for the increased nutritional needs of their wives.

There was a stark difference in the earnings of men from slum and rural areas with men from slum areas being at a disadvantage.

These findings reflect that in the slums of Delhi, migrants, who are invariably poor, illiterate or semi-literate are struggling hard to earn enough to meet the basic needs of life. In juxtaposition, in rural areas of Delhi, couples are economically, educationally and socially better off.

For most rural couples (91.3%), Delhi had been their native place, while couples from slums were from Uttar Pradesh (48.8%), Haryana (1.2%), Rajasthan (15%), Bihar (20%), Odisha (1.2%), West Bengal (5%), Uttaranchal (2.5%), and Ranchi (1.2%), Kolkata (1.2%), Madras (1.3%), Delhi (1.3%) and rest (1.3%) of them did not respond.

In rural areas, joint families are the norm (77.5%) while in urban slums nuclear families are a frequent occurrence (53.8%). Further, nearly three fourths of the rural couples were from joint families, couples from slums largely had nuclear families. In rural areas, mostly couples had their own house while in slums most families were on rented accommodation. Rural women have frequently adopted small family norm while women from slums often have more than two children. Educated girls tend to get married at appropriate age while illiteracy is linked to early marriage or child marriage. In slum areas, age at marriage of the couples had been lower than those in rural areas, where mostly marriages are done after reaching the legal age (of 18 years in case of females and 21 years for males). No locale-wise difference was seen in women's first pregnancy, which was generally a couple of months after their marriage.

More women from slums had their first child before the age of 19 years in comparison to rural women. More than one fourth of rural women underwent Caesarian section (operation) while nearly 82% women from slums had normal delivery. The reason for this could be economic constraints faced by women from slums to go to private clinics for delivery who prefer Caesarian deliveries. Cases of stillbirth and infant-death were more frequently reported from slum communities. Also, women from urban slums more frequently had underweight newborns than rural women. Further, women from nuclear families in urban slums tend to have babies with lower weight birth, which may be due to lack of adequate economic and physical support provided to them during pregnancy.

Utilization of maternal healthcare services is significant for healthy mothers and their newborn children. Husband-participation in maternal healthcare of their wives ensures proper usage of maternal healthcare services. Almost all the women availed antenatal care (ANC visits, TT injection and Acid tablets) services. Factors that facilitated utilization of antenatal care services are proximity to residence and free of cost availability. On usage of maternal healthcare services there was no difference between women from rural and slum areas. Interestingly, more rural women went for institutional deliveries and delivery at home was preferred by many women from slums. Healthcare staff like ANM and ASHA workers showed inclination to visit rural households while ignoring the poor urban slums, where they are needed the most. In slum areas, women generally had low level of awareness on family planning measures and healthcare staff also is less motivated to visit them and provide the requisite information. As a consequence, there is low level of usage of family planning methods in slum areas and couples have more children.

Rural women are more open to adoption of family planning methods after their first child birth than their counterparts in urban slums. There is a significant difference among rural and urban women on overall utilization of maternal healthcare services.

Regarding awareness on maternal healthcare programmes, like Janani Suraksha Yojana, rural and urban women were equally ignorant. However, on maternal healthcare services, rural women had more knowledge than urban women. As poverty and economic constraints were more prominent in urban slums, a few women from slums did not get adequate nutritional diet during pregnancy. They had to do heavy household work during pregnancy because of lack of support. They more frequently had to fetch water from outside (a heavy work, which is often avoided during pregnancy).

Women who had extra nutritional diets during pregnancy are able to deliver healthy children with normal birth weight. Food intake, quality as well as quantity, was linked to not only awareness, but also husband's / family's monthly income. In rural areas, women got more help from other family members in managing household work. In joint families, pregnant women were spared from doing heavy work while in urban slums pregnant women from nuclear families continued heavy household work.

In slum areas health centers/dispensaries are available within one km range while in rural areas many women had to travel longer distance to access health services. There was no difference between area of women and rest time during pregnancy.

Thus, the findings of the present study clearly show that socio-cultural (age at marriage, faith in traditional *dais*, restriction of food, etc.), socio-economic (income, type of house, nutritional intake, etc.), environment (household work, fetching water from outside the home, etc.) and political factors (availability of health services, behavior of medical staff members, etc.) influence the health of mothers and their new born children, as well as availing proper maternal healthcare services. Above-mentioned factors are intra and extra familial factors that influence women in accessing maternal healthcare services and somehow they also have a bearing on husband-participation in maternal healthcare of their wives.

Men, educated or illiterate, rural or urban, across religion and caste identities, presented themselves as more caring and supportive in contrast to their wives' perceptions.

Communication between husband and wife is the crux of their relationship. More than a half of women frequently shared information and feelings related to antenatal, natal and post natal care. It is required to address the culture of silence to increase discussion on and adoption of family planning methods between couples.

In contrast to the urban couples, rural couples have fared better in views about husband- support in maternal healthcare. They communicated more effectively. Men from rural Delhi have more frequently provided support—physically, economically and information- wise to their wives in comparison to men from urban slums. This was reflected in greater satisfaction levels among rural women with their husbands' support.

Decision-making by women in a family is an indicator of her importance and empowerment. It is assumed that joint decision- making by the couple is the best option. Quite interestingly, least number of women made decisions on issues related to maternal health. That means, on the matters related to women's own body, health and life, someone else (mainly mother-in-law/ husband) made decisions. Since in urban slums, families are often nuclear, women here had greater decision-making roles in household matters than those in rural areas where joint families were in domination. There is area-wise difference among men on their perceived roles and responsibilities as husbands with regard to maternal healthcare. One fourth of rural men did not recognize their role in pregnancy, delivery and after-care while 42.5% men from slum areas remained silent on this aspect. Roles perceived by men on maternal healthcare range from providing help in household chores, offering emotional support to participating in each and every stage of ante-natal care like escorting to health center to being present at the time of delivery, etc.

Scheme no.5.01 Facilitator and Inhibitor factors of husband-participation in maternal healthcare

The below schema no. 5.01 depicts various facilitator factors that contribute towards promoting husband-participation in maternal healthcare

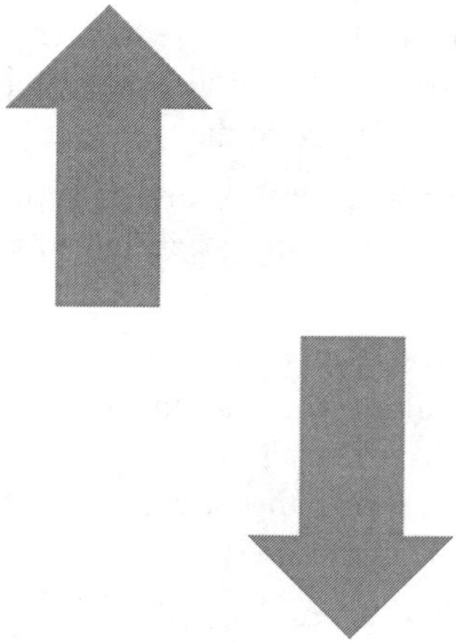

of their wife. Likewise, inhibitor factors reflect a decline in husband-participation in maternal healthcare services.

Facilitator factors in husband-participation in maternal healthcare

-Women from rural areas

Higher physical support (Standard Residual= + 3.6)

Higher perception on husband support on maternal healthcare (Standards Residual = +2.7)

-Couples from rural areas

Higher physical support (Standard Residual = +2.3)

Higher economic support (Standard Residual= +2.1)

Higher overall husband-participation (Standard Residual= +2.3)

Higher perception on husband support on maternal healthcare (Standards Residual = +3.1)

Inhibitors factors in husband-participation in maternal healthcare

-Women from slum areas

Lower physical support (SR= +2.0)

Lower perception on husband support on maternal healthcare (Standard Residual = + 2.7) Lower use of maternal healthcare services (Standard Residual = +3.4)

-Husbands from slum areas

Lower level of physical support (Standard Residual = +2.3)

-Couples from slum areas

Lower physical support (Standard Residual= +3.1)

Lower overall husband-participation in maternal healthcare (Standard Residual= +2.3)

Lower perception on husband support on maternal healthcare (Standard Residual = +3.2)

Suggestions

Suggestions to enhance maternal and child healthcare from social work point of view are presented. The study results reflect the significance of husband-participation in enhancing maternal healthcare. Husband-participation ensures better maternal health service utilization and provides emotional and physical support to the pregnant wife, enabling her to successfully pass through the developmental crisis of pregnancy and childbirth. In the cases where husband's participation was not there, women were found to skip ANC visits and ignore their health and emotional needs. This has irreparable negative consequences on the newborn. Based upon the study findings following suggestions are delineated:

- There is a need to sensitize family members in joint family especially mother-in-law and other elderly people about the significance of husband-participation in maternal healthcare.
- In the study, women's decision-making on matters related to their own health and body (when to conceive, which family planning method to use, etc.) is very low. Awareness related to women's right to have control over their body and life needs to be created among women as well as among their family members.
- Patriarchal norms act as hurdles to husband-participation. Rigid notions of masculinity do not allow men to help their pregnant wives in household work or provide emotional support to them. This aspect needs to be targeted and changed through application of strategies of social marketing and behavior change communication.
- Role-model couples can be identified at the community level and appreciated publicly for others to follow.
- Self-help groups of pregnant and lactating women can be formed at the community level. Similar groups of would-be and new-fathers may increase their participation and positive role at home too.
- In the study a few respondents expressed their discontent over the demeaning attitudes and rude behavior of doctors and healthcare

staff. Doctors and paramedical staff should be sensitized and trained to deal with couples going for maternal healthcare. The healthcare staff should provide comfortable environment in which the couples, especially from urban slums can feel free to ask questions related to pregnancy and child care. Doctors should encourage and involve men in their wife's pregnancy care. They should take couple counseling sessions on maternal healthcare rather than just talking to pregnant ladies.

- Through regular refresher trainings, healthcare staff should be motivated to encourage husband-participation in maternal healthcare.
- In some cases, in urban slums it was reported that ANMs and ASHA workers skip visits to pregnant ladies. Strict monitoring and supervision is required to avoid such situations.
- Though coverage of health services is good, best practices in maternal healthcare need to be documented, propagated and replicated.
- Study results have shown that child marriage and teen pregnancy are more frequent among girls who have not gone to school. Completing school and college education plays a significant role in preventing early marriage and early childbearing among women. Girls' education should be promoted and ensured.
- In the study awareness on maternal healthcare schemes such as JSY was very low. Efforts are required to enhance visibility, awareness and usage of these schemes.
- National health programmes and schemes have target-based approach, which is strictly monitored at the grassroots level. The ambit of focus on maternal healthcare services (like ANC visits, immunization, etc.) should also include indicators on husband-participation.
- Husband-participation in maternal healthcare should be one of the components of gender sensitization programmes. "Men make the difference" has been a tag-line of WHO-UNDP programmes aimed at targeting patriarchal notions in an amicable way and to encourage men to shoulder responsibility in reproductive and sexual health of their partners. In these programmes the old concept of manhood (perpetrator, aggressive, violent) was replaced with a new image (loving, caring, protecting, supporting).

- Usage of family planning methods to maintain adequate childbirth spacing should be popularized through awareness campaigns, social marketing and behavior change communication strategies.
- Through program media (songs, slogans, street theater) optimum usage of maternal healthcare schemes and also husband-participation should be advocated and popularized. Kilkari is one such noteworthy initiative by the government. Helplines, SMS alerts have been successful in ensuring effective service utilization in the field of HIV/AIDS and would also be beneficial in maternal healthcare.
- Maternity centers within one km range should be made available so as to promote service utilization and ensure the target of full institutional delivery.
- Besides ensuring quantitative targets (for instance, number of pregnant women enrolled, number of children immunized, etc.), equal attention needs to be paid to qualitative data (such as encouraging husbands to be more responsive, couple communication on family planning, birth spacing, etc.).
- Efforts should be made to ensure husband-participation at every stage and by every stakeholder. As many men were not able to accompany their pregnant wives to maternal health services due to job constraints, flexible timings such as evening or weekend meeting/consultation with doctors can be arranged.
- In situations where female health visitors face hesitation (due to cultural milieu), male health visitors can be appointed, who would be better able to deliver messages on family planning, etc.
- In western countries, it is the normative practice for husbands to be present in the labor room during their wife's delivery, such a system in India may be helpful in making men more sensitive towards their wife's needs and problems during pregnancy and delivery and may promote their participation.
- Posters, charts, pamphlets and other awareness materials should have pictures of couples (rather than women alone) so as to promote husband-participation.
- Government should prepare Information, Education and Communication (IEC) materials which focus on encouraging the husband-wife communication on maternal healthcare. While preparing the health communication material, focus should be given to illiterate population. IEC materials should reflect husband-

participation in each and every component of maternal healthcare and should also highlight benefits of the same for the health of mothers and their children.

- Sustainable development goals also give due importance to maternal and child healthcare. However, participation of men or husbands has not been stressed. Indicators of husband-participation should be included in maternal healthcare under the sustainable development goal 3 for preventing or reducing MMR and IMR.

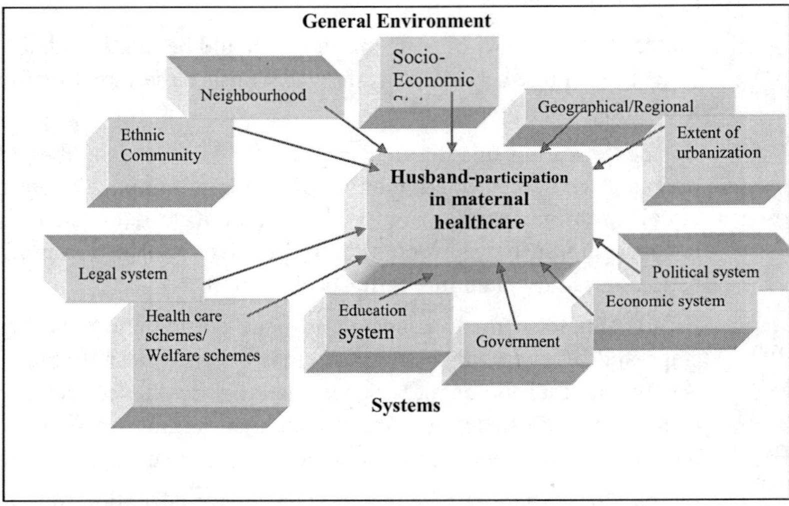

Diagram no. 501 Ecological model of family with husband-participation in maternal healthcare.

Social work interventions can be instituted in various settings such as hospitals, dispensaries, health centers, community centers, etc. NGOs and civil society organizations should also play an important role. Greater participation of husbands in maternal healthcare of their wives, in the long run, can be helpful in reducing the maternal deaths in the country. It would also be helpful for better health of the mother and her newborn child.Social work interventions based on Ecological Model of Family System are discussed as below:

The above diagram (no. 5.01) shows that husband-participation in maternal healthcare is influenced by the general environment like ethnic community and more directly reflected through family structure, practices, patterns and family dynamics, neighborhood, socio-economic status, geographical location, rural-urban area and various systems like legal, health, education, government, economic and political systems. All these systems play a significant role in ensuring husband-participation in maternal health.

To promote maternal healthcare, the scope of social work intervention is vast. Social workers should aim to promote factors that facilitate husband-participation and utilization of maternal healthcare services and minimize hindering factors. The diagram below (no. 5.02) presents the target groups/ stakeholders and roles of social workers-The above table no. 5.01 shows the scope of social work intervention for promoting husband-participation

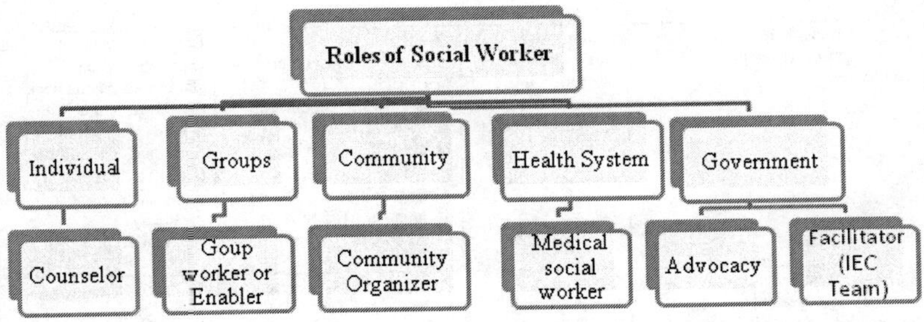

Diagram no. 5.02 Roles of social worker with various stakeholders

in maternal healthcare. Social work interventions are from micro to macro levels. The findings of the study indicate a strong need of medical social workers especially in maternal healthcare unit at primary, secondary and tertiary levels of healthcare systems. Based on the present research work, social work interventions are categorized into five parts as discussed below:

Individual approach:- A few men and women, in the study, had rigid patriarchal attitudes that acted as a hurdle in husband-participation. Case work and counseling with such individuals is required.

Couple counseling:- Social workers can do couple counseling in a wide range of situations at the preventive, promotive and ameliorative levels and also emphasize the importance of husband-participation in maternal healthcare.

Table no. 5.01 Social work interventions to promote healthy husband-participation in maternal healthcare

Objectives	***Target group***	***Session***	***Methods (optional/ use any)***
To understand the significance of husband-participation in maternal health care for their wife and newborn child	Individual (man and woman)	Impact of participation and non-participation in maternal healthcare	Face to face interaction Individual counseling Use of informative booklet (based on pictures with written information) Discussions Use of visual (posters), audio, audio-visual aids

(Contd...)

To create awareness about the pregnancy care, delivery care, after delivery and newborn child care	Couple Groups (women and men) Family Community Employees (at workplace)	Pregnancy care (nutritional intake, rest medicines, vaccination, etc.) Delivery care Post-natal care (includes child care) Couple communication related to antenatal, natal, post-natal & family planning Joint decision-making on household and maternal healthcare Symptoms and complications related to pregnancy and delivery Child immunization	Face to face interaction Couple counseling Use of informative booklet (based on picture with written information) Role play Use of visual (posters), audio, audio-visual aids, street play Observe nutrition day, vaccination day for pregnant women and children and institutional delivery day Feedback records by couples
To provide couple friendly health centre services related to maternal health care	Health system Health provider (doctor, ANMs, Asha worker, etc.) *Anganwadi* workers	Positive approach for husband-participation in maternal healthcare Separate waiting room with informative materials Meeting of doctor with couples Alternative time/modification of timing of ANC and child immunization	Face to face interaction Group discussion Use of information booklet (based on pictures with written information) Role play Use of visual (posters), audio, audio-visual aids, street play Feedback records by couples
To develop and disseminate information, education and communication materials	Government Communication development team	Ensure the accessibility and availability of maternal healthcare services in different languages and also to cater to the needs Focus on messages related to responsibility sharing by couples, age of child bearing, birth-spacing, etc. Significance of husband's presence at the time of delivery	Research reports Advocacy Use of various means of mass media

Group approach:- Family counseling or group counseling can be done to resolve tricky issues by social workers. For creating sensitization on husband-participation and participation of other family members in the care of pregnant ladies, sessions with families can be held. Even at the workplace, such sessions for awareness-generation can be held for men and women. In the community too (both rural and urban), such group sessions would go a long way in ensuring better care of women during pregnancy and after childbirth.

Health personnel:- Group sessions with formal (ANMs, ASHA workers) and informal (mother-in-law, other family members) systems can be held to improve services delivery and utilization of maternal healthcare services.

Awareness and Information, Education and Communication (IEC):- Social workers can be involved in preparing health education communication materials that may cover right or proper age of child-bearing, birth-spacing, usage of family planning methods, significance of couple communication, joint decision-making, and husband's support and participation in maternal healthcare. While developing IEC materials related to maternal healthcare Health Belief Model of health communication can be used as the framework for providing appropriate knowledge to target audiences (individual, couple, family, community, etc.). The stages of this model are discussed below with the aims of promoting husband-participation in maternal healthcare.

Perceived susceptibility:- IEC materials may cover risks/complications related to non- participation of husband in maternal healthcare. Perceived susceptibility has better ability to create need for desired action (here, husband-participation).

Perceived severity:- This stage highlights that content of message should also focus on impact of risk or complications. For example, non-participation of husband in pregnancy-care may have ser ious implications on the health and life of wife and children.

Perceived benefits:- This stage emphasizes that content of communication materials cover the benefits of husband-participation in maternal healthcare for wife and newborn child in terms of their health and well-being. For example, benefits or advantages of husband-participation in maternal healthcare include fewer instances of ill-health, better utilization of maternal healthcare services, healthy mother and newborn.

Perceived barriers:- This stage states that contents of communication materials should reflect that potential barriers such as social, self, economic, health system, etc., influence the behavior and practice of husband-participation in maternal healthcare.

Cues action:- This stage highlights the creation of mass level awareness about husband-participation in maternal healthcare through use of IEC materials.

Self-efficacy:- This is the last stage when the husband gains confidence to take responsibility to support and participate in maternal healthcare for his wife and child.

Hopefully the present research work would help in curbing some of the factors that fuel maternal mortality rate and infant mortality rate so that every mother and newborn child enjoys the right to life and healthy motherhood/childhood. It may provide greater insight to would-be parents and new parents to share responsibilities together so as to provide a conducive environment for their child for his/her optimum growth and development. It may also help in re-designing the existing maternal healthcare services and programs to ensure greater husband-participation.

References

Acharya, D.R., Bell, J. S., Simkhada, P. Teijlingen, E. R. V. & Regmi, P. R. (2010). Women's Autonomy in Household Decision-Making: A Demographic Study in Nepal. *Reproductive Health*, Vol. 7(15), pp.1-12. Retrieved on 7 January, 2015 from www.reproductive-health-journal.com/content.

Acharya, R. & Sureender, S. (1996). Inter-Spousal Communication, Contraceptive Use and Family Size Relationship Examined in Bihar and Tamil Nadu. *The journal of family welfare*, Vol. 42, No. 4, pp. 5-11.

Agarwal, P., Singh M. M. & Garg, S. (2007). Maternal Health-care Utilization among women in an urban slum in Delhi. *Indian Journal of Community Medicine,* Vol. 32, No. 3, pp. 203-205. Retrieved on 23rd January, 2013 from http://www.indmedica.com/ journals. php? journalid = 7&issueid = 101&articleid = 1378& action = article.

Archana, S., Nikhil, S.V., Singh, A.K. Palanivel, C. & Nongkynrih, B. (2010). Maternal Health Outcomes among Utilisers of Antenatal Services in an Urban Resettlement Colony of Delhi: A Record Based Descriptive. *Indian Journal of Maternal and Child Health*, Vol. 13(2), pp. 1-9. Retrieved on 12 August, 2011 from https:// sites.google.com/a/ijmch.org/www/home/previous-online-journals/volume-11-1.

Allendorf, K. (2007). Couples' Reports of Women's Autonomy and Health-Care Use in Nepal. *Studies in Family Planning,* Vol. 38 (1), pp. 35-46. Retrieved on 6th December, 2012 from http://www.jstor.org/stable/20454382 .

American Association for World Health, (1998). *Invest in the Future, Support Safe Motherhood* (p.48). Washington, D.C.: AAWH. In Padma, G.R. (2005). *Men's participation in reproductive health: A study of some village in Andhra Pradesh.* Kerala: Achutha Menon Centre for Health Science Studies (AMCHSS).

Awasthi, S., Nandan, D., Mehrotra, A.K. & Shankar, R. (2008).Male Participation in Maternal Care In Urban Slums Of District Agra. *Indian Journal of Prevention Social Medicines*, Vol. 39 (3&4), pp. 181-183. Retrieved on 1st December, 2015 from http:/ /medind.nic.in/ibl/t08/i3/iblt08i3p181.pdf.

Azimi, Y. N. & Atiya, A.S. (2003). Husband-Wife Communication and Family Planning Practices among Malay Married Couples In Mukim Rusila, Terengganu. *Medical Journal Malaysia,* Vol. 58 No 2, pp. 218-228. Retrieved on 22nd May, 2012 from http://www.ncbi.nlm.nih.gov/pmc/articles/PMC3245422/pdf/1742-4755-8-36.pdf?tool=pmcentrez.

Barnes, Linday (2007, December). Women's Experience of Childbirth in Rural Jharkhand. *Economic & Political Weekly*, vol. 42 No. 48, pp. 62-70.

Barua, A. (1998). Young Husbands Involvement in Reproductive Health in Rural Maharashtra. In Raju, S. & Leonard, A. (Editors) (2000). *Men as Supportive Partners in Reproductive Health*. New Delhi: Population Council. Retrieved on 7th July, 2011 from www.popcouncil.org/pdfs/menaspartners.pdf.

Barua, A., Pande, Rohini P., Macquarrie, Kerry & Walia, Sunayana (2004, December). Caring Men? *Economic & Political Weekly*, Vol. 39 No. 52, pp. 5661- 5668.

Bawah, A. A. (2002). Spousal Communication and Family Planning Behavior in Navrongo: A Longitudinal Assessment. *Studies in Family Planning,* Vol. 33(2), pp. 185-194. Retrieved on 18 July, 2012 from http://www.jstor.org/stable/3181172.

Bawa, Shilipi. (2003). Women's Reproductive Health in an Urban Slum (A Study of Kusumpur Phari Slum). Unpublished Manuscript. Department of Social Work, University of Delhi.

Becker, S., Becker, F.F. & Yglesias, C. S. (2006). Husbands' and Wives' Reports of Women's Decision-Making Power in Western Guatemala and Their Effects on Preventive Health

Behaviors. *Social Science & Medicine*, Vol. 62, pp.2313–2326. Retrieved on 16 July, 2013 from www.elsevier.com/locate/socscimed0277-9536/$.

Beegle, K., Frankenberg, E. & Thomas, D. (2001). Bargaining Power within Couples and Use of Prenatal and Delivery Care in Indonesia. *Studies in Family Planning*, Vol. 32(2), pp. 130-146. Retrieved on 21 May, 2015 from http://www.jstor.org/stable/2696342.

Berhane, A., Biadgilign, S, Amberbir, A., Morankar, S., Berhane, A. & Deribe, K. (2011). Men's Knowledge and Spousal Communication about Modern Family Planning Methods in Ethiopia. *African Journal of Reproductive Health*, Vol. 15 (4), pp. 24-32. Retrieved on 4 September, 2013 from http://www.bioline.org.br/pdf?rh11047.

Bhatta, D.N. (2013). Involvement of males in antenatal care, birth preparedness, exclusive breast feeding and immunizations for children in Kathmandu, Nepal. BMC Pregnancy and Childbirth, Vol. 13 (14), pp.1-7. Retrieved on 21st May, 2015 from http://www.biomedcentral.com/1471-2393/13/14.

Block, C.R, Norr, K. l., Meyering, S., Norr, J.L. & Charles, A.G. (1981). Husband Gate Keeping in Childbirth. *Family Relations,* Vol. 30(2), pp.197-204. Retrieved on 21 May, 2015 from http://www.jstor.org/stable/584131.

Bloom, S. S., Wypij, D. & Gupta, M. D. (2001). Dimensions of Women's Autonomy and the Influence on Maternal Healthcare Utilization in a North Indian City. *Demography*, Vol. 38 (1), pp. 67-78. Retrieved on 21 March, 2012 http://www.jstor.org/stable/3088289.

Boland, R. (1997). Promoting Reproductive Rights: A Global Mandate. New York: The Centre for Reproductive Law and Policy.

Cairo Programme of Action (September, 1994). *International Conference on Population and Development.* Retrieved on 18th April, 2011 from http://www.un.org/ecosocdev/geninfo/populatin/icpd.htm.

Carter, M.W. (2002). Because He Loves Me': Husbands' Involvement in Maternal Health in Guatemala. *Culture, Health & Sexuality*. Vol. 4, No. 3, pp. 259-279. Retrieved on 18th May, 2011 from http://www.jstor.org/stable/4005236.

Carter, M.W. & Speizer, I. (2005). Salvadoran Fathers' Attendance at Prenatal Care, Delivery, and Postpartum Care. *Journal of Public Health*. Vol. 18, No. 3, pp. 148-156. Retrieved on 18th May, 2011 from http://journal.paho.org/uploads/1137437675.pdf.

Census of India (2011). *District Census Handbook of Delhi – Village and Town Wise Primary Census Abstract (2014).* Series- 8 & Part-XII-B. Directorate of Census Operation, Delhi. Retrieved on 5th October, 2015 from http://www.censusindia.gov.in/2011census/dchb/DCHB%202011Concepts%20&%20 Definitions % 20Village % 20 and %20Town%20Directory.pdf.

Chowdhary D. Paul (1995). Chapter-4 Maternal and Child Health (pp. 45-49). *Child development/welfare* (4th edition).Delhi: Atma Ram & Sons.

Chandha, V. K. (1989). A Study of Maternal Factors in Relation to Outcome of Pregnancy in a Resettlement Colony of Delhi. Unpublished Manuscript. Faculty of Medical Sciences, Department of Preventive and Social Medicine, University of Delhi.

Danforth, E. J., Kruk, M.E., Rockers, P.C., Mbaruku, G. & Galea, S. (2009). Household Decision-making about Delivery in Health Facilities: Evidence from Tanzania. *Journal Health Population Nutrition*, Vol. 27(5), pp. 696–703.

Davis, J., Luchters, S. & Holmes, W. (2013). Men and Maternal and Newborn Health: Benefit, Harms, Challenges and Potential Strategies for Engaging Men. *Compass:*

Women's and Children's Health Knowledge Hub. Melbourne Australia. Retrieved on 19th January, 2014 from http: //mencare. org/ data/Men % 20 and % 20 Maternal % 20 and % 2 0Newborn % 20 Health % 20-% 20 Australia. pdf.

Development in practice (May, 1996). Chapter-2 The Socio-cultural Context (pp. 45-66). *Improving Women's Health in India*, by World Bank, Washington, D.C. ISBN-0-8213-3602-9.

Dodoo, F. N. A., Ezeh, A.C. & Owuor, T. O. (2001). Some Evidence against the Assumption That Approval of Family Planning Is Associated with Frequency of Spouses' Discussion of the Subject. *Population Studies*, Vol. 55 (2),pp. 195-198. Retrieved on 18 July, 2012 from http://www.jstor.org/stable/3092963.

Drennan, M. (1998). *Reproductive Health: New Perspective on Men's Participation*. Population Reports, Series J, No. 46.

Dutta, M. (2002). A Study on Male Participation in Reproductive and Child Health in an Urban Slum in Delhi. Unpublished Manuscript. Department of Community Health Administration, The Faculty of Medical Sciences, University of Delhi.

Dyson, Tim & Moore, M. (1983). On Kinship Structure, Female Autonomy and Demographic Behavior in India. *Population and Development Review*, Vol.9, No.1, pp. 35–60.

Edmonds, J. K., Paul, M. & Sibley, L.M. (2011). Type, Content, and Source of Social Support Perceived by Women during Pregnancy: Evidence from Matlab, Bangladesh. *Journal Health Population Nutrition,* Vol. 29(2), pp.163-173. Retrieved on from https://www.ncbi.nlm.nih.gov/pmc/articles/PMC3126989/.

Farooqui, M. N. I. (1994). Interpersonal Communication in Family Planning in Pakistan. The Pakistan Development Review, Vol. 33 (4), pp. 677-684. Retrieved on 18 July, 2012 from http://www.jstor.org/stable/41259787.

Feyisetan, Bamikale J. (2000). Spousal Communication and Contraceptive use among the Yoruba of Nigeria. *Population Research and Policy Review*, Vol. 19, No. 1, pp. 29-45. Retrieved on 22nd May, 2012 from URL: http://www.jstor.org/stable/40230256.

Furuta, M. & Salway, S. (2006). Women's Position within the Household as a Determinant of Maternal Healthcare Use in Nepal. *International Family Planning Perspectives*, Vol. 32 (1),pp. 17-27. Retrieved on 5 August, 2011 from http://www.jstor.org/stable/4147608.

Ganesh, Kamala (1997). Common Gynaecological Morbidity Pattern in Elderly Females. In Bagchi, Kalyan (Ed.): *Elderly Female in India*, New Delhi: Society for Gerontogical Research & Helpage India, pp.65-78.

Ghosh, Shanti (1996). Life Cycle of Maternal and Child Health. In Srivivasan, K. (edited), *Population Policy and Reproductive Health*, New Delhi: Hindustan Publication. Government of India. The All India Services (Leave) Rules (1955). pp. 1-31. Retrieved on 28th September, 2016 From http://intraips.gov.in/kms/ActsRules/Revised AIS Rule Vol I Rule 03.pdf.

Government of India. *Report (2005-06) on National Family Health Survey-III, Vol.-I.* Retrieved on 9th Feb. 2011 from http://hetv.org/india/nfhs/nfhs3/NFHS-3-India-Full-Report-Volume-I.pdf.

Government of India, Ministry of Health and Family Welfare. *Report (July, 2009) on Reproductive and Sexual Health of Young People of India.* Retrieved on 17th Feb. 2012 from http://mohfw.nic.in/NRHM/Documents/RSH of YP in India.pdf.

Government of India, Ministry of Health and Family Welfare (2009). *Report (2005-06) on National Family Health Survey-III, Delhi*. International Institute for Population

Sciences: Mumbai. Retrieved on 17 Feb. 2012 from http://www.nfhsindia.org/NFHS 3%20Data/Delhi printed version for website.pdf.

Government of India. *Annual Report (2010-2011)*, Ministry of Health and Family Welfare. Retrieved on 13 Feb. 2012, from http://mohfw.nic.in/showfile.php?lid=951.

Government of India. *Report on Census of India 2011*. Retrieved on 27th January, 2012 from http://www.censusofindia.com.

Government of India, Ministry of Home Affairs (2011*). Directorate of census operations of Delhi.* Retrieved on 10th December, 2012 from http://www.censusofindia.com.

Government of India, Ministry of Health and Family Welfare (2007). *State of Urban Health of Delhi*. Urban Health Resource Centre: New Delhi. Retrieved on 17 Feb. 2012 from http://www.uhrc,in.

Government of India, Ministry of Housing and Urban Poverty Alleviation (August, 2010). *Report of the committee on slum Statistics/census*. Retrieved on 15th December, 2012 from http://www.mhupa.nic.in.

Government of India. *Census directory of rural village of Delhi 2011*. Retrieved on 10th December, 2012 from http://www.censusofindia.com.

Government of India (2014). *Statistical Abstract of Delhi.* Directorate of Economic and Statistics Retrieved on 10th December, 2016 from http://www.delhi.gov.in/wps/wcm/connect/f508bc8046667b0e9cf6bcf5a4ed47e7/Statti stical + Abstract + of + Delhi + 2014. pdf? MOD = AJPERES & lmod = 1346796026 & CACHEID = f508bc8046667b0e9cf6bcf5a4ed47e7.

Government of India. *Annual Report (2015-2016)*, Ministry of Health and Family Welfare. Retrieved on 10th March, 2017, from http://mohfw.gov.in/showfile.php?lid=4276.

Government of India, Ministry of Health and Family Welfare (2015-16). *National Family Health Survey-IV, India Fact Sheet*. International Institute for Population Sciences: Mumbai. Retrieved on 10th March, 2017 from http://www.rchiips.org/nfhs.

Government of India (2017-18). Union Budget of India. Retrieved on 10th March, 2017 from http://indiabudget.nic.in/ub2017-18/bh/bh1.pdf.

Gupta, J. A. (1996). Chapter -3 Gender Dimension of Social Relations in Healthcare –An Historical Overview (pp. 89-120). *New Freedom, New Dependencies: New Reproductive Technologies, Women Health and Autonomy*, Stichting De Zaaier: The Hague Leiden.

Haider, Raana. (1995). Chapter - Women and Nutrition and Health: The Input and the Output (pp.93-109). A perspective in Development, Bangladesh: University press limited.

Hazarika, Indrajit (2010). Factors that Determine the Use of Skilled Care during Delivery in India: Implications for Achievement of MDG-5 Targets. *Maternal child health journal,* DOI 10.1007/s10995-010-06873.Retrieved on 8th Oct. 2010 from http://www.springerlink.com/content/v022012159385p22/fulltext.pdf.

Helzner, Judith Frye (May, 1996). Men's Involvement in Family Planning. *Reproductive Health Matters*. Vol. 4, No. 7, pp. 146-154. Retrieved on 5th August, 2011 on from http://www.jstor.org/stable/3775363.

High Court of Delhi (2012). *Delhi Judicial Services (Leave) Rules, (2011).* pp. 1-43. Retrieved on 28th September, 2016 from *delhihighcourt.nic.in/writereaddata/upload/.../Notification File 0VC32GG8.PDF.*

Horstman, R. G., Nepal, B. & Pant, P.D. (2004). *Husband Involvement in the Prevention of Maternal Ill-health: the Determinants of Husband Domestic Support in Rural*

Low- land Nepal. Retrieved on 19th July 2011 from http://paa2004.princeton.edu/download. asp?submissionId=40758.

Hou, X. & Ma, N. (2013). The Effect of Women's Decision-Making Power on Maternal Health Services Uptake: Evidence From Pakistan. *Health Policy & Planning,* Vol.28, pp.176-184. Retrieved on 13 May, 2014 from http://heapol.oxfordjournals.org/content/28/2/176.full.pdf.

Human Impact Partners (2011). *Fact Sheet: Parental Leave and the Health of Infants, Children and Mothers.* pp. 1-5. Retrieved on 28th September, 2016 From www. humanimpact. org.

Iliyasu,Z., Abubakar, I.S., Galadanci, H.S.& Aliyu, M.K. (2010). Birth Preparedness, Complication Readiness and Fathers' participation in Maternity Care in a Northern Nigerian community. *African Journal of Reproductive Health,* Vol. 14(1), pp.21-32. Retrieved on 21 May, 2015 from http://www.bioline.org.br/pdf?rh10002.

Ijadunolal, M.Y., Abiona, T. C., Ijadunolal, K. T., Afolabi, O.T., Esimai, O. A. & OlaOlorun, F. M. (2010). Male Involvement in Family Planning Decision Making in Ile-Ife, Osun State, Nigeria. *African Journal of Reproductive Health,* Vol. 14 (4), pp. 45-52. Retrieved on 4 September, 2013 from.

International Institute for Population Science (IIPS) and Macro (2000). *National Family Health Survey –II, 1998-99*. Mumbai: IIPS.

Jayalakshmi, M.S., Ambwani, K., Prabhakar & Swain, P. (2002). A Study of Male Involvement In Family Planning. *Health and Population Perspectives and Issues*, Vol.25, No.3, pp. 113-123.

Jamuna, D. (1995). Ageing Women in India: A Profile, *Research and Development Journal*, Vol. 1 No. 3, pp. 3-14.

Jejeehoby, S. J. & Varkey, L. C. (2004). Maternal Health and Pregnancy-Related Care. In Jejeehoby, S. J. (edited), *Looking back Looking forward: A Profile Of Sexual And Reproductive Health in India*, Jaipur: Prem Rawat for Rawat Publication.

Jeffery, Roger & Basu, A. M. (1996). *Girls' Schooling, Women's Autonomy and Fertility Change in South Asia*. New Delhi: Sage Publications.

Kaida, A., Kipp, W., Hessel, P. & Kondelule, J. (2005). Male Participation in Family Planning: Results from a Qualitative Study in Mpigi District of Uganda. *Journal of Biosocial Science,* Vol. 37 (3), pp. 269-286. Retrieved on 16 July, 2013 from http://journals.cambridge.org/abstract S0021932004007035.

Karra, M. V., Stark, N.N. & Wolf, J. (1997). Male Involvement in Family Planning: A Case Study Spanning Five Generations of a South Indian Family. *Studies in Family Planning,* Vol. 28 (1), pp. 24-34. Retrieved on 4 July, 2011 from http://www.jstor.org/stable/2137968.

Kiani, K. & Framurz, M. (2003). Motivation and Involvement of Men in Family Planning in Pakistan. *The Pakistan Development Review*, Vol. 42 (3), pp. 197-217. Retrieved on 18 July, 2012 from http://www.jstor.org/stable/41260540.

Kakkar, Sudhir (1982). *Identify and Adulthood*, Delhi: Oxford University Press.

Kamal, N. (1999). Inter-Spousal Communication on Family Planning as Determinant of the use of Modern Contraception in Bangladesh. *The Journal of Family Welfare*, Vol. 45, No. 1, pp. 31-43.

Kausar, Rehana (2005). Maternal Mortality in India – Magnitude, Causes and Concerns. *Indian Journal for the Practicing Doctor*, vol. 2, no.2 (2005-05-2005-06). Retrieved on 29th Sept. 2010 from http://www.indmedica.com/journals. php? journalid = 3&issueid = 58&articleid = 722& action = article.

Kaye, D.K., Kakaire, O., Nakimuli, A., Osinde, M. O., Mbalinda, S. N. & Kakande, N. (2014). Male involvement during pregnancy and childbirth: men's perceptions, practices an experiences during the care for women who developed childbirth complications in Mulago Hospital, Uganda. *BMC Pregnancy and Childbirth*, Vol. 14 (54), pp. 1-8. Retrieved on 21 May, 2015 from http://www.biomedcentral.com/1471-2393/14/54.

Khan, M.E., Khan, I. & Mukerjee, N. (1997). Involving Men in Safe Motherhood. *The Journal of Family Welfare*. Vol. 43, No. 2, pp. 18-30.

Khan, M. E. & Patel, B.C. (1997). *Male involvement in Family Planning: A Knowledge, Attitude, Behavior and Practice Survey of Agra District*. New Delhi: Population Council. Retrieved on 31st July, 2011 from www.popcouncil.org/pdfs/frontiers/OR TA/Asia/india MI.pdf.

Khan, Z., Mehnaz, S., Ansari, M. A., Khalique, N. & Siddiqui, A.R. (2009). Existing Practices and Barriers to Avail of Maternal Healthcare Services in Two Slums of Aligarh. *Health and Population: Perspectives and Issues,* Vol. 32 (3), pp. 113-123.

Khanna, R., Kapadia, S. & Dongre, Lalita (1998). Men's Roles and Responsibilities for Women's Health. Vadodara: WSRC.

Koenig, M. A., Simmons, G.B. &. Misra, B. D. (1984). Reviewed Work Husband-Wife Inconsistencies in Contraceptive Use Responses. *Population Studies*, Vol. 38, No. 2, pp. 281-298. Retrieved on 22nd May, 2012 from URL: http://www.jstor.org/stable/2174077.

Kululanga, L. I., Sund by, J., Malata, A. & Chirwa, E. (2011). Striving to promote male involvement in maternal healthcare in rural and urban settings in Malawi - a qualitative study. *Reproductive Health,* Vol. 8(36) pp.1-12. Retrieved on 22nd May 2012 from http://www.reproductive-health-journal.com/content/8/1/36.

Kululanga, L. I., Sundby, J., Chirwa, E., Malata, A. & Maluwa, A. (2012). Barriers to Husbands' Involvement in Maternal Healthcare in a Rural Setting in Malawi: A Qualitative Study. *Journal of Research in Nursing and Midwifery,* Vol. 1(1) pp. 1-10. Retrieved on 21 May 2015 from http://www.interesjournals.org/JRNM.

Kumar, A. & Negi N. S. (No year). *Impact of Household Decision Making Power on Women Empowerment in India: Evidences from NFHS-3 survey*. Retrieved on from 6th December, 2012 from http://iussp2009.princeton.edu/papers/93418.

Kumar, P. & Singh, S. K. (No year). *Does Male Participation in Maternal Health Can Ensure Achieving MDGs in India? Evidences from National Family Health Surveys.* Retrieved on 15th April, 2011 from http://iussp2009.princeton.edu/downlo ad.aspx?s ubmissio nId=90930.

Kumar, S. (Nov. 1996). Involving the Men. *Seminar*, No. 447, pp. 39-42.

Lasee, A. & Becker, S. (1997).Husband-Wife Communication about Family Planning and Contraceptive Use in Kenya. *International Family Planning Perspectives*, Vol. 23 (1), pp. 15-20. Retrieved on 18 July 2012 from http://www.jstor.org/stable/2950781.

Lewis, S., Lee, A. and Simkhada, P. (2015). The Role of Husbands in Maternal Health and Safe Childbirth in Rural Nepal: A Qualitative Study. *BMC Pregnancy and Childbirth,* Vol. 15 (162), pp.1-10. Retrieved on 27 August, 2015 from http://www. biomedcentral.com/1471-2393/15/162.

Link, C. F. (2011). Spousal Communication and Contraceptive Use in Rural Nepal: An Event History Analysis. *Studies in Family Planning*, Vol. 42, No. 2, pp. 83–92. Retrieved on 22 June 2011 from http://onlinelibrary.wiley.com/doi/10.1111/j.1728-4465.2011.00268.x/pdf 27/1/2012.

Mahapatro, S. R. (2012). Utilization of Maternal and Child Healthcare Services in India: Does Women's Autonomy Matter?. *The Journal of Family Welfare*, Vol. 58 (1), pp.22-33.

Maharaj, P. (2000). Promoting Male Involvement in Reproductive Health. *AIDS: Global Concerns for Women*. Agenda, No. 44, pp. 37-47. Retrieved on 15 April 2011 from http://www.jstor.org/stable/4066433.

Mahmood, N. & Ringheim, K. (1997). Knowledge, Approval and Communication About Family Planning as Correlates of Desired Fertility Among Spouses in Pakistan. *International Family Planning Perspectives,* Vol. 23 (3), pp. 122-129. Retrieved on 18 July, 2012 from http://www.jstor.org/stable/2950768.

Manju.(2006). Utilization of Reproductive Health Services by Women in an Urban Slum of Delhi. Unpublished Manuscript. Department of Social Work, University of Delhi. Matthews, Z., Brookes, M., Stones, R. W. & Hossain, M. B. (2005). Village in the City: Autonomy and Maternal Health-Seeking Among Slum Populations of Mumbai. In Kishor, S. *A Focus on Gender: Collected Papers on Gender Using DHS Data.* Calverton, Maryland, USA: ORC Macro. Retrieved on 13th December, 2012 from https://dhsprogram.com/pubs/pdf/OD32/5.pdf.

Mekonnen, M. (2009). Husbands' Roles in Prenatal care In Addis Ababa. Unpublished Manuscript.Faculty of Social and Behaviour Sciences, University of Amsterdam, Netherland. Retrieved on 21 May 2015 from http://amma.socsci.uva.nl/theses/muleta.pdf.

Mihira, V. K., Nancy, N. S. & Joyce, Wolf (1997). Male Involvement in Family Planning: A Case Study Spanning Five Generations of a South Indian Family. *Studies in FamilyPlanning*, Vol. 28, No. 1, pp. 24-34. Retrieved on 4th July, 2011 from URL: http://www.jstor.org/stable/2137968.

Ministry of Health and Family Welfare (2003). *Reproductive and Child Health & Family Planning Programme Implementation Plan (PIP) Draft*. Department of Family Welfare, New Delhi: Ministry of Health and Family Welfare.

Ministry of Health and Family Welfare (2006). *National Programme Implementation Plan RCH Phase-II Programme Document.* Retrieved on 15th March, 2011 from http://mohfw.nic.in/NRHM/RCH/guidelines/NPIP_Rev_III.pdf

Ministry of Health and Family Welfare (2009). *National Family Health Survey-III (2005-06) of Delhi State Report.* Mumbai: International Institute for Population Sciences. Retrieved on 17th February, 2012 From http://hetv.org/india/nfhs/nfhs3/NFHS-3-Delhi-state-report.pdf.

Ministry of Health and Family Welfare (April, 2010). *Report on District Level Household and Facility Survey (2007-08) India*. Mumbai: International Institute for Population Sciences. Retrieved on 21st March, 2012 from http://www.rchiips.org/pdf/INDIA REPORT DLHS-3.pdf.

Ministry of Health and Family Welfare (2010). *Report on District Level Household and Facility Survey (2007-08) Delhi*. Mumbai: International Institute for Population Sciences. Retrieved on 21st March, 2012 from http://www.rchiips.org/pdf/rch3/state/Delhi.pdf.

Ministry of Women and Child Development (2010). *Indira Gandhi Matritva Sahyog Yojana (IGMSY)- A Conditional Maternity Benefit (CMB)Scheme.* New Delhi. Retrieved on 10th March, 2017 from http://wcd.nic.in/sites/default/files/IGMSYscheme.pdf.

Ministry of Health and Family Welfare (2011). *Family Welfare Statistic of India*. Retrieved on 13 Feb. 2012, from http://mohfw.nic.in/showfile.php?lid = 771.

Ministry of Health and family Welfare (2016). *MAA (Mothers' Absolute Affection) Programme for Promotion of Breastfeeding.* Retrieved on 10th March, 2017 from http://nrhm gov.in/MAA/Operational Guidelines.pdf.

Ministry of Health and family Welfare (2016). *Kilkari Message.* Retrieved on 10th March, 2017 from http://nrhm-mcts.nic.in/KKMSG.aspx.

Ministry of Health and family Welfare (2016). *Pradhan Mantri Surakshit Matriva Abhiyan.* Maternal Health Division, Government of India. Retrieved on 10th March, 2017 from https: // pmsma. nhp. gov. in/ wpcontent/ uploads / 2016/09/Pradhan Mantri Surakshit Matritva Abhiyan-2.pdf.

Mishra, A., Varkey, L.C., Ottolenghi,E., Das,A., Huntington, D. & Adamchak , S. (2002). *Men in Maternity Study: Results from the Pre-Intervention Survey of Pregnant Women and their Husbands at Three Intervention and of only Women at Three Control Employee's State Insurance Corporation Dispensaries in Delhi, India.* Population Council, Frontiers in Reproductive Health. Retrieved on 26th May, 2011 from http://www. popcouncil. org/pdfs/frontiers/MIM India long BL Jul02. pdf.

Mistry, R., Galal, O. & Lu, M. (2009). Women's Autonomy and Pregnancy Care in Rural India: A Contextual Analysis". *Social Science & Medicine*, Vol. 69, pp. 926-933. Retrieved on 3 May, 2014 from www.elsevier.com/locate/socscimed.

Mitchell, R. E. (1972). Husband-Wife Relations and Family-Planning Practices in Urban Hong Kong. *Journal of Marriage and Family,* Vol. 34 (1), pp. 139-146. Retrieved on 11 September, 2013 from http://www.jstor.org/stable/349641.

Mosha, I., Ruben, R., & Kakoko, D. (2013). Family Planning Decisions, Perceptions and Gender Dynamics among Couples in Mwanza, Tanzania: A Qualitative Study. *BMC Public Health,* Vol. 13 (523), pp.1-13. Retrieved on 2 September, 2013 from http://www.biomedcentral.com/1471-2458/13/523.

Mosunmola, S., Adekunbi, F. & Foluso,O. (2014). Women's Perception of Husbands' Support during Pregnancy, Labour and Delivery. *IOSR Journal of Nursing and Health Science,* Vol. 3 (3), pp. 45-50. Retrieved on 21 May 2015 from *www.iosrjournals.org.*

Moore, M. (1999). Men in Uttar Pradesh, India know little about women's Reproductive Health Needs. *International Family Planning Perspectives,* Vol. 25, No. 2, pp. 107. Retrieved on 21st May, 2011 from http://links. jstor.org/sic?sici= 01903187% 28199906 % 2925%3A2%3X107%3AMIU PIK%3E2.0CO%3B2-L.

Mukherjee, B. N. (1975). The Role of Husband-Wife Communication in Family Planning. *Journal of Marriage and Family*, Vol. 37, No. 3, pp. 655-667. Retrieved on 21st March, 2012 from URL: http://www.jstor.org/stable/350530 .

Mullany, B. C., Hindin, M. J. & Becker, S. (2005). Can Women's Autonomy Impede Male Involvement in Pregnancy Health in Kathmandu, Nepal? *Social Science and Medicine.* Vol. 61, pp. 1993-2006. Retrieved on 18th May, 2011 from www. elsevier. com/ locate/ socscimed.

Mullany, B. C. (2006). Barriers to and Attitudes towards Promoting Husbands' Involvement in Maternal Health in Kathmandu, Nepal. *Social Science and Medicine*. Vol. 62, pp. 2798-2809. Retrieved on 18th May, 2011 from www.elsevier.com/locate/socscimed.

Mullany, B.C., Becker, S. & Hindin, M. J. (2006).The Impact of Including Husbands In Antenatal Health Education Services On Maternal Health Practices In Urban Nepal: Results From A Randomized Controlled Trial. *Health Education Research.* Vol. 22, pp. 166-176.Retrieved on 13th April 2011 from her.oxfordjournals.org doi:10.1093/her/cyl060.

Mullick, S., Kunene, B & Wanjiru, M.(2005). Involving Men in Maternity Care: Health Service Delivery Issues. *Agenda: Special Focus on Gender, Culture and Rights* (special issue). pp. 124-135. Retrieved on 26th May,2011 from http://www. popcouncil. org / pdfs / frontiers /journals/Agenda Mullick05.pdf.

Mullany, B.C., Lakhey, B., Shrestha, D., Hindin, M.J. & Becker, S. (2009). Impact of Husbands' Participation in Antenatal Health Education Services on Maternal Health Knowledge. *Journal of Nepal Medical Association,* Vol. 48 (173), pp.28-34. Retrieved on 21 May, 2015 http://www.jnma.com.np/jnma/index.php/jnma/article/viewFile/191/ 673.

Nagdeve, Dewaram Abhiman (2008, December). Maternal Healthcare in Jharkhand. *The Journal Family welfare*, Vol.54, No. 2, pp. 40- 51.

Odhiambo, O. (1997). Participation in Family Planning Decisions in Kenya. *Population Studies*, Vol. 51, No. 1, pp. 29-40. Retrieved on 22nd May 2012 from URL: http:// www.jstor.org/stable/2175071.

Padma, G.R. (2005). *Men's Participation in Reproductive Health: A study of Some Village in Andhra Pradesh*. Kerala: Achutha Menon Centre for Health Science Studies (AMCHSS).

Padma, G. Rama (2005). Perceptions on Safe Motherhood: An Analysis of Results from Rural Andhra Pradesh. *Economic and Political Weekly*, Vol. 40, No. 5, pp. 465-473. Retrieved on 21st March, 2012 from http://www.jstor.org/stable/4416139.

Pandey, A., Roy, N., Sahu, D. & Acharya, R. (2004, February). Maternal Healthcare Services. *Economic & Political Weekly*, vol. 39 No. 07, pp. 713-720.

Park, K. (2002 & 2009).Chapter-2 Concept of Health and Disease, chapter-10 Preventive Medicine in Obstetrics, Paediatrics and Geriatrics (pp.362-365) and chapter-22Healthcare Of The Community (pp.791) *Textbook of Preventive and Social Medicine* (17th& 20th edition). Jabalpur (India): M/s banarisidas bhanot.

Pathak, K. B., Pandey, A. & Ojha, A. (2001). Child Spacing and the Utilization Maternal Healthcare Services in Some Selected State of India: An Analysis. *The Journal Family welfare*, Vol. 47, No.2, pp.18-25.

Pathi, S., Rosania, S. K., Bhalla, S. & Singh, S. (2004). Male Involvement in Family Planning Practices. *Health and Population Perspectives and Issues*, Vol. 27, No.3, pp. 166-172.

Pelon, N.J.P., Rob, U.&Khan, M.E. (1999). Chapter-5 Decision Makers and Chapter-6 Innovative Reproductive Health Programmes for Men. *In Men in Bangladesh, India and Pakistan (Reproductive Health Issues)*, India: Hindustan Publishing Corporation.

Pradhan, A., Khanna, R., Kukade, P. & Ubale, U. (2004). *Increasing Men's Involvement in Reproductive Health.* Vadodara: Society for Health Alternatives (SAHJ).

Radkar, Anjali & Parasuraman, Sulabha (2007, August). Maternal Death in India: An Exploration. *Economic & Political Weekly*, Vol.42 No. 31, pp. 3259-3263.

Raju, S. (1999). Men as Supportive Partners in Reproductive Health: NGOs Pave the Way. In Pachauri, S. (Editor). *Implementing A Reproductive Health Agenda In India: The Beginning*, New Delhi: Population Council.

Raju, S. & Leonard, A. (Editors) (2000). *Men as Supportive Partners in Reproductive Health*. New Delhi: Population Council. Retrieved on 7th July, 2011 from www.popcouncil.org/pdfs/menaspartners.pdf.

Rani, Sandhya, Ghosh, Saswata, & Sharan, Mona (2007, December). Maternal Healthcare Seeking among Adolescent Girls in Jharkhand. *Economic & Political Weekly*, Vol. 42 No. 48, pp. 56-61.

Razi, S. (June, 2012). Empowered Women, Empowered Nation. *YOJANA*, Vol. 56, pp. 24-27.

Registration General, (January, 2011). *Sample Registration System Bulletin (2009)*. Vital Statistics Division: New Delhi. Vol. 45, No.1. Retrieved on 13 Feb. 2012, from http://www.censusindia.gov.in/vital statistics/ SRS Bulletins / SRS % 20 Bulletin%20-% 20January % 202011. pdf.

Ross, N.J., Chruch, S., Hill, M., Seaman, P. & Roberts, T. (2012). The Perspectives of Young Men and Their Teenage Partners on Maternity and Health Services During Pregnancy and Early Parenthood. *Children & Society*, Vol. 26, pp.304-315. Retrieved on 02 September, 2013. DOI:10.1111/j.1099-0860.2010.00338.x002/09/2013.

Saini, N. K. & Singh, M. (2004). Awareness and practice of spacing methods in a Rural block of Haryana. *Perspectives and Issues,* Vol. 27 (1), pp.1-8.

Sample Registration System and Office of Registrar General (2013). *Special bulletin on Maternal Mortality in India*. Retrieved on 31st October 2015 from http://www.censusindia.gov.in/vital statistics/ SRS Bulletins/Final-MMR%20Bulletin-2007-09 070711.pdf.

Sagar, Alpana (2006). Chapter- 8 Doctors' Business or Women's Business? Towards Making Childbirth Safer for Poor Women in India. In Chawla, Janet. (edited), *Birth and Birth Givers: the Power behind the Shame*, New Delhi: HAR-Anand Publication.

Santhya, K.G.,Ram,U., Acharya, R., Jejeebhoy, S. J., Ram, F. & Singh, A. (2010). Associations Between Early Marriage and Young Women's Marital and Reproductive Health Outcomes: Evidence from India. *International Perspective Sexual Reproductive Health,* Vol. 36 (3), pp. 132-139. Retrieved on 21st March, 2012 from Stable URL: http://www.jstor.org/stable/20775350.

Sapkota, S., Kobayashi, T. & Takase, T. (2012). Husbands' Experiences of Supporting their Wives during Child Birth in Nepal. *Midwifery,* Vol. 28(1), pp. 45-51. Retrieved on 16th July, 2013 from www.elsevier.com/midwdoi:10.1016/j.midw.2010.10.010.

Sapkota, S., Kobayashi, T., Kakehashi, M., Baral, G. & Yoshida, I. (2012). In the Nepalese context, can a husband's attendance during childbirth help his wife feel more in control of labour?. *BMC Pregnancy and Childbirth,* Vol. 12 (49), pp.1-10. Retrieved on 21st May, 2015 from http://www.biomedcentral.com/1471-2393/12/49.

Secka, E. (2010) Men's Involvement in Care And Support during Pregnancy and Childbirth A Qualitative Study Conducted in The Gambia. Unpublished Manuscript. Department of General Practice and Community Medicine Section for International Health, University of Oslo. Retrieved on 21 May 2015 from https://www.duo.uio.no/bitstream/handle/10852/30026/EbbaxSecka.pdf?sequence=1.

Shahamfar, J., Kishor, J. & Shokhvash, B. (2007). Effect of Educational Intervention on Male Participation in Family Planning in Iran. *Health and Population-Perspectives and Issues,* Vol. 30 (4), pp. 292-299.

Sharan, M. & Thomas, W. V. (2002). Spousal Communication and Family Planning Adoption: Effects of a Radio Drama Serial in Nepal. *International Family Planning Perspectives*, Vol. 28 (1), pp. 16-25. Retrieved on 18 July, 2012 from http://www.jstor.org/stable/3088271.

Sharma, R. K. (2010, June). New Born Care among Tribes of Central India: Experiences from Micro Level Studies. *Social change*, vol. 40 No. 2, pp. 117 -137.

Sharma, R. & Desai, S. (1992). Vitamin A in Pregnancy: A Review. *Indian Journal of Maternal and Child Health,* Vol. 3, No.2, pp. 36-40.

Sherpa, H. & Rai, D. (1997).Safe Motherhood is a Family Responsibility. *Report on National Safe Motherhood Awareness Campaign*, pp. 72. Kathmandu, Nepal: Centre for Development and Population Activities. In Padma, G.R. (2005). *Men's*

Participation in Reproductive Health: A Study of Some Village in Andhra Pradesh. Kerala: Achutha Menon Centre for Health Science Studies (AMCHSS).

Singh, K. K., Bloom, S. S. & Tsui, A. O. (1998). Husbands' Reproductive Health Knowledge, Attitudes, and Behavior in Uttar Pradesh, India. *Studies in Family Planning*, Vol. 29, No. 4, pp. 388-399. Retrieved on 4th July, 2011 URL: http://www. jstor. org/stable/172251.

Singh, A. & Arora, A.K. (2008). How Much Do Rural Indian Husbands Care for the Health their Wives'. *Indian Journal of Community Medicine,* Vol. 33, No.1, pp. 19-25. Retrieved on 25th May, 2011 from http://www.ijcm.org.in.

Singh, D., Lample, M. & Earnest, J. (2014). The involvement of men in maternal healthcare: cross-sectional, pilot case studies from Maligita and Kibibi, Uganda. *Reproductive Health,* Vol. 11 (68), pp.1-8. Retrieved on 27 June, 2016 from http://www. reproductive - health - journal. com/ content /11/ 1/ 68.

Singh, S. & Ram, F. (2007). Husbands' Support to Wives in Accessing Reproductive Health Services: A Gender Perspective from Rural India. *Women's Link*, Vol. 13 (4), pp. 16 to19.

Sinha, Kounteya (2012, April 9). 25% Births by Untrained Hands. [*The Times of India*], p.10, D1- D2.

Sinha, Kounteya (2013, November 30). UK Mums, Dads Can Share Leave to Care for Babies. [*The Times of India*], p.20, D1- D4.

Sosten, C., Paul, K. K., Jack, R.M. & Robert, K. (2015). A study on factors hindering husbands from participating in maternal healthcare in Malawi. *African Journal of Nursing and Midwifery,* Vol. 2 (1), pp. 66-75. Retrieved on 20 February, 2017 from ype=application/pdf&op=1.

Srivastava, H.C. (2011). Chapter-12 Determinants of Male Involvement as Supportive Partners in Women's Reproductive Health. In Ram, F., Unisa, S. & Sekher, T.V. (Editors). *Population, Gender and Reproductive Health,* Jaipur: Rawat Publication.

Story, W. T., Burgard, S.A., Lori, J.R., Taleb, F., Ali, N.A. & Hoque, D.M. E. (2012). Husbands' involvement in delivery care utilization in rural Bangladesh: A qualitative study. *BMC Pregnancy and Childbirth,* Vol. 12 (28), pp.1-12. Retrieved on 5th May, 2015 from http://www.biomedcentral.com/1471-2393/12/28.

Story, W.T. & Burgard, S.A. (2012). Couples' reports of household decision-making and the utilization of maternal health services in Bangladesh. *Social Science & Medicine*, Vol. 75, pp. 2403-2411. Retrieved on 3 May, 2014 from www.elsevier.com/locate/ socscimed.

Team TOI (2017, February 2). *Health Scan: Treatment doesn't Match Diagnosis*. [*The Times of India*], p.11, D1- D2.

The Time of India (2016, June 12). *One Woman Dies Every Five Minutes during Pregnancy: WHO.* Retrieved on 10th January, 2017 from http://timesofindia. indiatimes. com/city/ mumbai/ One-woman-dies-every-5-minutes-during-pregnancy-WHO/articleshow/52715015.cms.

Tinkew, J. B., Ryan, S., Carrano, J.A & Moore, K.A. (2007). Resident Fathers' Pregnancy Intentions, Prenatal Behaviors, and Links to Involvement with Infants. *Journal of Marriage and Family*, Vol. 69 (4), pp. 977-990. Retrieved on 12 September, 2013 from http://www.jstor.org/stable/4622502 .

Thaddeus, S. & Maine, D. (1994). Too Far to Walk: Maternal Mortality in Context. Social Sciences and Medicine, Vol. 38, No.8, pp. 1091-1110.

Thapa, D.K. (2012). Woman's Autonomy And Husband's Involvement In Maternal Healthcare Utilization In Nepal. Unpublished Manuscript. Department of Social Sciences Sociology of Consumers and Households, Wageningen University.

Thapa, D.K. & Niehof, A. (2013). Women's Autonomy and Husbands' Involvement in Maternal Healthcare in Nepal. *Social Science & Medicine,* Vol. 93, pp.1-10. Retrieved on 16 July, 2103 from www.elsevier.com/locate/socscimed.

Tweheyo, R., Lule, J.K., Tumwesigye, N.M. & Sekhandi, J.N. (2010). Male Partner Attendance Of Skilled Antenatal Care in Peri-Urban Gulu District, Northern Uganda. *BMC Pregnancy and Childbirth,* Vol. 10 (53), pp. 1-9. Retrieved on 21 May, 2015 Retrieved on 21 May, 2015 Retrieved on 21 May, 2015 http://www. biomedcentral. com/1471-2393/10/53.

United Nation (1996). Chapter-4 Strategic Objectives and Actions © Women Health (p 56 – 73). *The Beijing Declaration and the Platform for Action (Fourth World Conference on Women Beijing, China 4-15 September 1995).*New York: United Nations Department of Public Information.

United Nations General Assembly, Report of the Ad Hoc Committee of the Whole of the Twenty-first Special Session of the General Assembly *Key actions for the further* implementation of the programme of action of the International Conference Population and Development [A/S/-21/5/Add.1]. New York, 1999: paragraph 62(c). Retrieved on 15th April, 2011 from http://whqlibdoc.who.int/hq/2002/WHO FCH RHR 02.3. pdf.

United Nations Fund for Children. (1998). *The State of the World's Children: Focus on Nutrition*. New York: UNICEF.

United Nations Children's Fund (Feb. 2012). *The State of the World's Children 2012.* Retrieved on 2nd March, 2012 from http://www.unicef.org/sowc/files/SOWC 2012 Main Report EN 21 Dec 2011. pdf.

United Nation Development Programme (2015). *Sustainable Development Goals.* Retrieved on 13 March, 2016 from http://www.undp.org/content/dam/undp/library/ corporate/brochure/SDGs Booklet Web En.pdf.

Varkey, L.C., Huntington, D., Das, A. et al. (2002). *Involving Men in their Wives' Antenatal And Postpartum Care in India.* New Delhi: Population Council. Retrieved on 26th May 2011 from http://www.popcouncil.org/pdfs/frontiers/MIM India long BL Jul02. pdf.

Viterif, E. (1994). The Consequences of Iron Deficiency and Anaemia in Pregnancy on Maternal Health. *The Foetus Infant Science News*, Vol. 11, pp. 14-18.In Padma, G.R. (2005).*Men's Participation in Reproductive Health: A Study of Some Village in Andhra Pradesh*. Kerala: Achutha Menon Centre for Health Science Studies (AMCHSS).

Vermeulen, E., Miltenburg, A. S., Barras, J., Maselle, N., Elteren, M.V. & Roosmalen, J.V. (2016) Opportunities for male involvement during pregnancy in Magu district, rural Tanzania. *BMC Pregnancy and Childbirth*, Vol. 16 (66), pp.1-9. Retrieved on 20 February, 2017 from http://download.springer.com/static/pdf/959/ art%253A10.1186%252Fs12884-01608538.pdf?originUrl=http%3 A%2F% 2Fbmcpregnancychildbirth.biomedcentral.com%2Farticle%2 F10.1186%2 Fs128840160853 8&token2=exp=1 487583928~acl=% 2Fstatic%2Fpdf%2F 959%2Fart%25253A1 0.1186%25252Fs12 88401608538.pdf* ~hmac=e1ca896ab 9226d3975db528c2ce1 306c6484aa72401dd0d2b 09a59eca6f22856.

Wai, K.M., Shibanuma, A., Oo, N. N. , Fillman,T. J., Saw, Y. M. & Jimba, M. (2015). Are Husbands Involving in Their Spouses' Utilization of Maternal Care Services?: A Cross-Sectional Study in Yangon, Myanmar. *PLoS ONE*, Vol. 10 (12) pp. 1-13. Retrieved on 4 July 2016 from http://journals.plos.org/plosone/article/ asset?id=10.1371%2Fjournal.pone.0144135.PD F.

Woldemicael, G. & Tenkorang, E. Y. (2010). Women's Autonomy and Maternal Health-Seeking Behavior in Ethiopia. *Maternal and Child Health Journal,* Vol. 14, pp.988–

998. Retrieved on from 21st May, 2015 from li*nk.springer.com/article/10.1007/s10995-009-0535-5.*

World Health Organization. (1971). Technical Report Series, No.483. In Park, K. (2009). *Textbook of Preventive and Social Medicine* (20th edition).Jabalpur (India): M/s banarisidas bhanot.

World Health Organization (2000). *Health Aspects of Maternity Leave and Maternity Protection, Statement to the International Labour* Conference, 2 June 2000. Retrieved on from http://www.who.int/reproductivehealth/publications/maternal mortality 2000/ Health aspects of maternity leave.en.html; 2303-204.

World Health Organization (2002). *Programming For Male Involvement In Reproductive Health*: Report of meeting of WHO Regional Advisors in Reproductive health. Geneva: World Health Organization. Retrieved on 15th April, 2011 from http://whqlibdoc.who.int/hq/2002/WHO FCH RHR 02.3.pdf.

World Health Organization (2015). *Trends in Maternal Mortality: 1990 to 2015. Geneva: WHO Document Production Services. Retrieved on 10th March, 2017 from apps. who. int/iris/bitstream/10665/194254/1/9789241565141 eng.pdf*.

World Health Organization (2016). *Factsheets: Maternal Mortality.* Retrieved on 22nd December, 2016 from http://www.who.int/mediacentre/factsheets/fs348/en/.

Yargawa, J. & Leonardi-Bee, J. (2015). Male Involvement and Maternal Health Outcome: Systematic Review and Meta-Analysis. *Journal of Epidemiol Community Health,* pp.1-9. Retrieved on 21 May 2015 from http://jech.bmj.com/content/early/2015/02/19/jech-2014-204784.full.pdf+html.

Zewditu, K. T. (2002). Husband-Wife Communication About Family Planning in Assosa Town (Ethiopia). Unpublished Manuscripts. Department Of General Practice & Community Medicine, University Of Oslo. Retrieved on 4 September, 2013 from https://www.duo.uio.no/bitstream/handle/10852/30082/tessema.pdf?sequence=1.

Index